COLORADO WILDSCAPES

Bringing Conservation Home

*A garden can be a pleasure, a personal sanctuary
that nurtures and sustains you, even as you nurture it.
A garden can bring you home, reconnecting you to the intricate
community of life that animates this beautiful Earth.*

—Susan J. Tweit,
Rocky Mountain Garden Survival Guide

Audubon At Home in Colorado

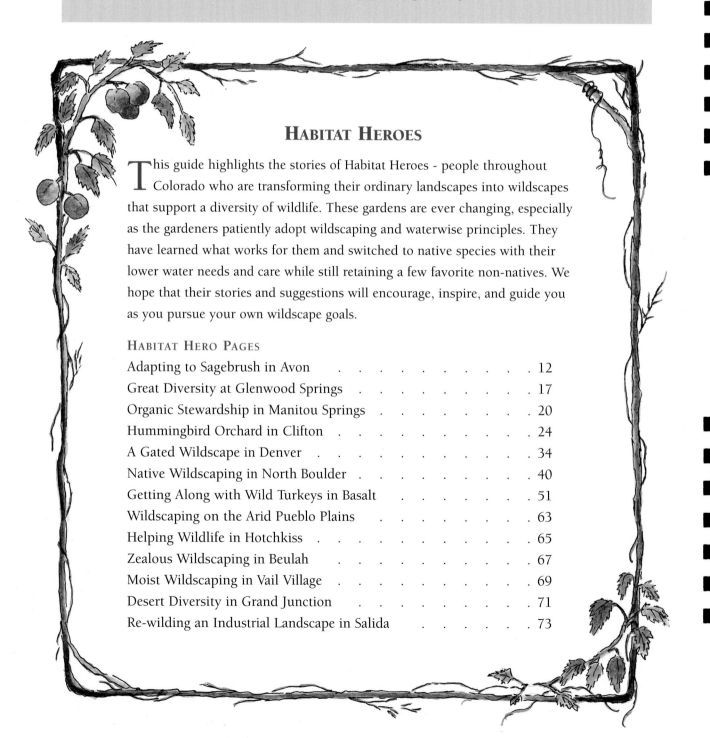

HABITAT HEROES

This guide highlights the stories of Habitat Heroes - people throughout Colorado who are transforming their ordinary landscapes into wildscapes that support a diversity of wildlife. These gardens are ever changing, especially as the gardeners patiently adopt wildscaping and waterwise principles. They have learned what works for them and switched to native species with their lower water needs and care while still retaining a few favorite non-natives. We hope that their stories and suggestions will encourage, inspire, and guide you as you pursue your own wildscape goals.

HABITAT HERO PAGES

CONTENTS

Credits

Printed in Canada by: Friesens

Distributed by: Westcliffe Publishers - *www.westcliffepublishers.com*

Designer: Ann Green, Green Design

Front Cover photos: Western Tanager ©Wendy Shattil/Bob Rozinski; all others Bob Johnson

Illustrations: Susie Mottashed except where indicated.

Back Cover photos: Towhee ©Wendy Shattil/Bob Rozinski, Science Class Cathryn O'Connor

INTRODUCTION
A Bird's-Eye View of Colorado

The spectacular landscapes of Colorado and the Rocky Mountain region are home to an equally jaw-dropping diversity of birdlife, including an array of species that are found nowhere else on earth. According to Bird Conservation (April 2004), at least half the world's population of Brown-capped and Black Rosy-Finches and Clark's Nutcrackers call this region home. The numbers of Broad-tailed and Calliope Hummingbirds and MacGillivray's Warblers are higher here than anywhere else on earth. And almost all of the world's Gunnison Sage-Grouse make their home in the sagebrush country of western Colorado.

Sharing Colorado's open spaces with this chorus of birds is a stunning variety of other animals and plants that once surprised and even baffled the pioneers who arrived here from the humid east. Depending upon where you live today, you might expect to see pronghorns and prairie dogs, damselflies or Cutthroat Trout, box turtles, prairie clover, aspen or cacti - each perfectly suited to one or another of the state's many microclimates and life zones.

Clark's Nutcracker is found in high country and depends heavily on pine seeds. Stephen Jones

Unfortunately for many of these species, the habitats that they are so well adapted to have been altered dramatically by rapid human population growth over the past two centuries. As our population has sprawled across Colorado landscapes, we have redesigned the land and water to suit our own needs, often with no thought about the impacts on the birds and other wildlife that were living here long before we arrived. The houses we build are landscaped to provide us with a little refuge from the daily stress of modern life, and with little consideration for how they fit into the broader landscape. Our yards represent a great simplification of the habitats they have replaced, resulting in a dramatically reduced diversity of plants and animals that can reside there. What if we took a remarkably different view of our yards and gardens? What if we saw them not as places that separate us from the surrounding world but as special landscapes that actually connect us to the rest of nature - our own private gateways to the exuberant life that is all around us?

If each of us treated our patch of land as an integral part of the larger habitat and invited wild birds and other creatures to share that space with us, the landscapes around our homes could fill our need for refuge in an even more meaningful way: providing a refuge for both us and our wild neighbors, a place that reconnects us to the natural world and contributes to our own sense of wellbeing. This is precisely the aim of **Audubon At Home**.

Opposite page: Bob Johnson

The Audubon At Home Connection

Audubon At Home is a program for optimists - people who believe that the things they do can have positive impacts on the world around them - people like you who know that their own yard is a place where they can get closer to nature because it's a part of the vibrant web of life that surrounds us. Just because you believe these things and are sure that you want to make your yard a link to the wilder world, it isn't always obvious how to proceed. That's where *Colorado Wildscapes*, the Audubon At Home guide for Colorado, comes in.

Through this guide, you'll learn some easy steps that you can take to become an active steward of your yard or garden as a unique piece of the biosphere. The Audubon At Home program begins with recognizing that we can make more room for flapping wings and paw prints in our yard by simply softening our own footprints on the earth: by reducing the demands we make on our natural resources - especially through water and energy conservation - and reducing or eliminating any damaging effects of our own activities. This includes minimizing the use of pesticides and other toxic chemicals, protecting water quality by preventing chemical run-off or soil erosion, and controlling invasive plants that might escape our yards and seriously alter wild habitats.

But the most exciting outcomes of Audubon At Home come with the giant strides we can make to build positive connections between our own property and the surrounding landscape by cultivating native plants and creating mini-habitats for native birds and other wildlife right in our own backyards. As it turns out - and as you will see again and again in the pages that follow - what's good for birds, butterflies and other wildlife tends to also be good for people. Transforming our yards from highly managed lawns and gardens to wilder landscapes can also keep our maintenance costs and efforts down, while creating endless opportunities for every member of the family to enjoy and learn about nature. And we can do all of this while maintaining a landscape that is attractive, fun and exhilarating by using an approach to backyard stewardship known as **Wildscaping**.

Any individual yard or garden may seem relatively insignificant as a wildlife habitat, but according to the EPA, residential lawns (not including parks, businesses, or industrial areas) cover some 20 million acres in the United States. Imagine if all of those yards were transformed into small habitat patches. The additional wildlife habitat would be comparable to increasing the area of the entire National Wildlife Refuge system by twenty percent. While this mosaic of backyards could not provide all the same values to wildlife as an equivalent unbroken wilderness, the wildlife benefits would still be enormous. Our backyard wildscapes could contribute meaningfully to our broader conservation goals in Colorado by providing needed rest and refueling stops for migratory birds on their way to larger, wilder landscapes. That's the promise and the potential of Audubon At Home.

Wildscaping in Colorado

Wildscaping - creating healthy, diverse habitats that include native plantings to feed, shelter, and nurture wild creatures - is a fun and exciting way to truly bring conservation home. When you turn your yard into a wildscape, you're drawing on the wisdom of wild places to create a living space around your home for a diverse array of species to thrive as your neighbors. A healthy wildscape is an interactive community of species filling many different roles - eating, growing, reproducing, recycling - right at your doorstep.

Wildscaping builds healthy communities - both human and wild - by nurturing the natural webs of interconnected lives, from tiny ants to shimmering dragonflies and brilliant Western Tanagers. Wildscaping helps restore our place in nature and our connection to this Earth that is our home. And rediscovering these connections is one of the most important things we can do to keep ourselves and our world healthy and sane.

Wildscaping is practical, too. Colorado is a challenging state for gardeners because of its high elevation, temperature extremes, intense sunlight, sporadic precipitation and desiccating winds. All of these factors tend to aggravate the generally arid conditions that prevail in most parts of the state. Without helpful guidance, newcomers and long-time residents alike often have difficulty adjusting to the realities of living in this high-elevation semi-desert. By following the principles in *Colorado Wildscapes*, you can learn to be water-wise and be in tune with your local environment as you plant and care for your yard.

Whether you're the steward of a large acreage, a suburban yard, or a container garden on an apartment balcony, you can help improve habitats for Colorado wildlife by becoming a wildscaper. In your important role as steward of a precious piece of Colorado earth - part-time habitat restorer, part-time wildlife manager - you can help achieve the Audubon At Home goal of conserving and restoring habitat all across America for our native birds and other wildlife, one yard at a time.

Using this Habitat Guide

This *Colorado Wildscapes* habitat guide offers a wealth of specific information that will help you design, maintain and enjoy your own wildscape, whether you're a veteran gardener or a beginner. First, review the Colorado Wildscape Regions beginning on page 61 to determine the habitat where you live. Old hands then will want to go straight to specific sections that cover their area of interest. Beginners can step through the process by starting with Exploring Your Wildscape Site on page 9. Then read How Wildscapes Work on page 14 to quickly learn the way wild communities grow and function, thus becoming aware of the general wildscaping principles that will guide you. Finally, delve into the details of forming a habitat in Designing and Building Your Wildscape on page 29, preparing you to put all your plans into action.

While this habitat guide is designed specifically for Colorado, much of the general information can also be applied elsewhere in the Rocky Mountain region. Because of the wide variation in Colorado's climate and topography from place to place, we take a regional approach to wildscaping, tailoring recommended plants and practices to the specific region where you live in the state. Plants and animals are referred to by their common names and no scientific names are included in the body of the text. However, you can find the full scientific names of native plant species as well as all other plants mentioned in the text beginning on page 74.

Wildscaping - from meadows lush with seasonal blooms to more formal neighborhood landscapes. It's a personal choice that also supports wildlife.
David Winger

The text generally refers to yards and backyards, but the principles and practices of wildscaping are equally applicable to both smaller and larger landscapes, from rooftop gardens and schoolyards to shopping malls and other commercial properties. Similarly, the guide focuses on wildscaping and waterwise or Xeriscape (landscaping for water conservation) practices for sustaining birds, but the general principles and many practices are equally beneficial to a wide variety of other wildlife, from bats and salamanders to butterflies, dragonflies and other invertebrates.

Additional information is listed in the final reference sections. To delve further into Audubon At Home, please visit the National Audubon Society's website at *www.audubon.org*. Audubon Colorado's website *www.auduboncolorado.org* includes regularly updated information on *Colorado Wildscapes* plus places to share your wildscape experiences with others.

If you get excited at the sight of a swooping hawk above your house or thrill to the songs of katydids and kingbirds in your garden, then you've come to the right place. Welcome to Audubon At Home. Come join us in the adventure of building wildscapes all across Colorado. You'll be helping wildlife, improving your community and discovering a lot of fascinating things about yourself and the natural world. Get the kids involved too! And don't forget to just have fun!

1

EXPLORING YOUR WILDSCAPE SITE

Before embarking on your wildscaping adventure in your own backyard, it's important to have a clear picture of the basic concepts involved in successful wildscaping. Knowing your site - your wildscape zip code, your local variation of the general climatic conditions, and soil type - is crucial to your planning, designing and ultimately your on-the-ground success. Details of these wildscaping basics make up much of the remainder of this habitat guide.

Colorado Wildscape Regions

Learning your wildscape zip code: the first step in planning a successful Colorado wildscape is to identify where you are located within these major regions - your wildscape zip code - because their differing climate and soil conditions dictate the kinds of plant and animal communities that can thrive within each. It's important for you to understand the differences among the state's wildly divergent geographic and ecological regions, from high mountains to grassy plains and semi-desert shrublands. Much of the state is semi-arid and most moisture comes from winter and spring snowfall, making water the limiting factor for both wildlife and landscaping. The mountains accumulate extra moisture by wringing rain and snow from moisture-laden clouds rising to pass over the peaks, but winters are severe and the frequent winds taxing, especially to birds. Plains grasslands and semi-desert shrublands are some of the driest and hottest habitats in the state.

Yellow-headed Blackbird is a colonial nester using cattails found in marshy habitats.
© Wendy Shattil/Bob Rozinski

This habitat guide divides the state into six major wildscape regions based on characteristic plant communities and birds, including five Wildscape Regions and the Riparian/Wetland Wildscape Zone, which occurs within all regions. Although wildscape regions are similar to other habitat classification systems, such as biogeographic regions and life zones, they aren't exactly the same. They represent a more simplified approach to classifying Colorado's natural landscapes, for wildscaping purposes, enabling us to tailor some of our recommendations to specific regions of the state without creating a level of complexity that gets in the way of easily using this guide.

When you're ready to create your wildscape and identify your region, please refer to the Colorado Wildscape Regions beginning on page 61. Accompanying each wildscape region is a story about a Habitat Hero who has been successful in that region.

Where is Your Habitat?

To determine which wildscape region you live in, take some walks through natural areas near your home and observe the kinds of plants that are growing there. Is the dominant plant community a forest, a grassland or a shrubland? Which species dominate or are most obvious?

Broad-tailed Hummingbird on Sunset Hyssop.
Lynn & Bruce Bowen.

Next, identify exactly where you live within your wildscape region. Are you close to another region and do you experience some of the conditions that are more typical of that area? This kind of information will help you in determining what species of plants you can reasonably expect to thrive in your landscape, as well as the wildlife you can potentially attract. In the mountain communities, particularly above 8,500 feet, shrubs become important since only a few trees will survive. Note nearby habitats like marshes, streams, undeveloped habitat, urban settings with or without mature landscaping, large open water areas. These will play a role in how you develop your wildscape.

Don't despair if you live in an urban area. Inner city locations attract wildlife too! The Denver Botanic Gardens is home to Rock Wrens and Red Foxes; and if you plant penstemon and agastache species or California Fuchsia, you will provide an energy stopover for hummingbirds as they migrate through this habitat in late summer. But even in an urban area you need to know your wildscape zip code before you can successfully transform your yard into a home for native wildlife.

Xeric plants like these penstemons in Denver and the agastache (top) in the Basalt foothills provide fueling stops for migrating hummingbirds. Panayoti Kelaidis

What are Your Yard's Microclimates?

In addition to understanding the details of your site's exposure to sun, wind, moisture and temperature extremes, try to understand the micro-variations within the site itself. One portion may be mostly sunny, while another is largely in deep shade. Your house can have a big impact on microclimates: plants located close to the north side experience much colder and moister conditions than those that are close to the hotter, drier south side.

What's Your Soil Type?

Before doing any planting, take a little time to get to know what your soil is like. In Colorado's mountains, valleys, and mesas soil textures vary from gravelly through sandy to silty, while clay is the predominant soil type in Front Range landscapes. Clay absorbs water slowly and loses it to evaporation and drainage slowly. Sand does the opposite. If you need help in assessing your soil needs, you can contact your County Extension office, the local outreach of Colorado State University's agricultural and garden programs, for assistance. Visit their web site at: *www.ext.colostate.edu*.

Consider Your Family Lifestyle, Too

So far we've considered the wildlife assets and limitations of your yard, based on the constraints created by climate and soil. But let's not forget about how your family wants to use your landscape: the kids need a place to play and the family likes to barbecue. Maybe you need shelter from some of our sunniest, hottest weather? Think also about the outside view from inside your house.

Adding a fence encloses an area into an outdoor room, especially when you incorporate a wooden bench and whimsical accents. If you have a shed or building, accent one outside wall with birdhouses and sculptures, then enclose this new room with lattice and plantings. Invite the birds in by hanging feeders or nesting pouches. Fill terra cotta pots with Pincushion Flower, Butterflyweed, Blue Flowering Salvia and fall asters to welcome butterflies.

With little supplemental water, plants such as Shrubby Cinquefoil, Jupiter's Beard, yarrow and salvias thrive. Bob Johnson

TIP: Pick up a large pinch of dry soil and roll it between your fingers. How does it feel? Gritty? Smooth? Hard? Lumpy? Loose? Now dampen it and pinch it between your fingers. Can you squeeze it into a long ribbon? Does the ribbon break up? Or does the wet soil just crumble? Soil that feels smooth and silky when dry (or is one hard lump) and forms a ribbon when wet is predominantly clay. If it is gritty when dry but forms a bit of a ribbon when wet, it's probably silty with some sand. If the dry soil is just grainy and it crumbles when wet, it's sandy.

MEET A HABITAT HERO:
ADAPTING TO SAGEBRUSH IN AVON

Pearl gardens for the love of being outdoors. "Gardening relaxes me and is less stressful than playing the games of golf and tennis." Her gardens are seemingly on top of the world, with scenic vistas to the New York peaks in the Sawatch Range.

Eagle County - Semi-Desert Shrubland Pearl Taylor

DILEMMA: At 8200 feet, you imagine a Montane setting with aspens and firs. This is not the case in this Avon setting with its sunny, windy, and natural dry sagebrush landscape making it a huge gardening challenge to overcome. Over the last ten years Pearl has created a landscape with a delightful array of mini-gardens ranging from dry riverbed plantings to a desert-like cacti garden to an extensive "bluff" planted as a mini forest that adds vertical interest and privacy. A turf-type Tall Fescue lawn is weed-free and seemingly well adapted to mountain conditions in resisting the dandelions that infiltrate bluegrass lawns.

PROVIDING DIVERSITY: The gardens are dotted with birdhouses, seed and woodpecker suet feeders and several water features. Pearl recommends planting natives such as rabbitbrush, bitterbrush and sagebrush since they are adapted to the poor soil and fluctuating temperatures. Berms were created to host Rocky Mountain Junipers, Piñon and Bristlecone Pines. Shrubbery includes Saltbush, thimbleberry, buffaloberry, gooseberry and Red Currant.

WILDSCAPING TIP: Deer are a major nuisance, along with small ground squirrels and chipmunks. Pearl tries different remedies every year and has had some success with Liquid Fence®. Her maintenance tip is to "pull a weed immediately when you see it...else the task will become too much." Higher elevations create short frost-free gardening, so create protected garden areas with later-blooming plants to extend the growing season.

FAVORITE PLANT: Moonshine Yarrow is a particular favorite since "deer don't eat it" and the mustard yellow blooms last for weeks and "can be deadheaded all at once." A favorite native shrub is Antelope Bitterbrush for its attractive yellow spring blooms and seeds for the birds.

Draw a Site Sketch

Draw a sketch of the existing features of your landscape including house and buildings, borders, wet areas, exposure and slope changes and existing bird feeding areas. Map every major feature, even if you're not sure whether it's really significant. Include:

⮞ Trees, shrubs (show relative heights and sizes of clumps: short, medium, tall)

⮞ Dead trees (snags), brush piles, rocky outcrops

⮞ Evergreen hedges, shelterbelts, rock walls - these can provide wind protection for bird feeders

⮞ Lines of shrubs that can serve as protected travel corridors for wildlife

⮞ Water sources such as wells, spigots, existing sprinkler system

⮞ Prevailing wind direction, location of sheltered areas for summer butterflies and winter birds

⮞ Sites that warm up quickly in the spring for early starting plants

⮞ Views to preserve by not planting tall vegetation

⮞ Also note any conditions on adjacent land that could affect your wildscape:

⮞ Neighboring trees extending into or shading your yard

⮞ Open field for grassland species - for instance, a place to locate bluebird houses

⮞ Major water area, like a pond, highly desirable habitat that will attract new species to your yard

⮞ Any source of disturbance where you might plant or construct a barrier

⮞ Busy road - avoid food plants that attract animals to this hazard

EXISTING LANDSCAPE

Susan J. Tweit

It's also helpful to make a list of seasonal wildlife visitors including what features and vegetation attracts them. If your neighbor has more birds, check to see what features and plants are THE attractants.

2

HOW WILDSCAPES WORK: BUILDING YOUR HABITAT

A diverse habitat has many designs as reflected in the urban landscape (above) and the aspen glen (below). Above: Panayoti Kelaidis

Layer by layer, step by step, let your garden be the teacher revealing that each one of us can be a habitat steward, a caretaker, by welcoming birds, butterflies, toads and dragonflies into a healthy yard teeming with life. Your yard is a private place and also part of a much larger landscape and a regional ecosystem. Think about how your own wildscaping can complement and enhance neighboring landscapes. Most animals require more space than is found in a single backyard and are very mobile. Walk nature trails for design ideas by looking at the naturalized groupings of plants, including what species grow where, how they fit into the landscape and relate to each other, as well as what wildlife can be found there.

Variety is essential in your design and plantings: trees, dense shrubs and ground covers that provide year-round fruit, berries, seeds - these are the key to having your own wild kingdom. Consistency in providing basic wildlife needs is essential, too; off-and-on, part-time provisions can lead to disappointment. Try to incorporate waterwise planning (see page 35) into your design to benefit regional water resources while helping to increase the available habitat for local wildlife.

Keep in mind that there is no single ideal, no exact formula for success. Become familiar with the wildscaping materials; then pick and choose to suit your tastes and budget. When you view your wildscape as habitat, you'll begin to look at plants differently. Your yard will go beyond just being pretty to being bountiful as well.

Let your plants grow naturally for the most visual and wildlife benefits. Crew-cut pruning looks unnatural and also diminishes fruit and seed harvests. Winter brings especially keen silhouette viewing if you take the time to look - and the wavering seed heads of grasses and perennials provide essential food for small seedeaters such as juncos and finches. Many factors go into making a truly attractive year-round wildscape, so let your imagination run free!

Above all, don't rush: take time to build your wildscape gradually, plant by plant and layer by layer. Working slowly allows you to pace yourself and gives you time to witness the exciting results of each new change you make. Even small steps can result in big outcomes. A single new plant species may attract a new kind of wildlife. Take time to enjoy each new success - to learn from your wildscape and apply the lessons - and, of course, to smell the wild roses.

Jim Hawkins

Creating Shelter and Diversity

At the most basic level, your wildscape provides a safe and secure living space for the creatures that are attracted to it. Even before you concern yourself with providing food and water for your wild guests, you can begin to think about those elements that will provide a sense of security for them. What kind of vegetative structure can you bring to your site that will provide protection from the sun, wind and storms? How can you create places where a small bird can hide from a predator, or lookouts where a flycatcher can perch between foraging flights?

The key is to build vertical structure and diversity into your wildscape with many different layers and densities of vegetation. A landscape that consists only of a lawn will only attract a few species that might feed on the ground, and they won't stick around very long without a nearby shelter to escape to. When you add shrubbery, you multiply its value to wildlife manifold. And if you add additional layers of vegetation with trees of different sizes and groundcovers beneath the shrubs and trees, you create the foundation for a dynamic and attractive wildscape. If you're limited by height restrictions, plant fast growing annual vines on arbors to provide a bird's-eye view.

This Plains wildscape provides the needed diversity in layered vegetation to support the needs of most wildlife. Connie Holsinger

Choose from these wildlife friendly, moderate to low-water selections, according to your wildscape region:

- Tall Trees: Ponderosa Pine, Piñon Pine, Burr Oak
- Mid-size Trees: Rocky Mountain Maple, Rocky Mountain Juniper
- Shrubs: Rabbitbrush, Leadplant, Threeleaf sumac, Mountain Ninebark, Fernbush
- Vine: Trumpet Vine - good hummingbird plant
- Perennials: Chocolate Flower, Dotted Gayfeather, Blanket Flower
- Annuals: salvia, California Poppy, or Scarlet verbena for hummers
- Grasses: Switchgrass, Side-oats Grama

You can also increase the wildlife value and interest of your wildscape by incorporating horizontal structure and diversity - variations in plantings and vegetation structure as you move across your yard from one side to the other: a clump of bushes here, a tall tree there, a perennial flowerbed in between and an un-mowed meadow beyond. Plant Wild Plum to form tangled sheltering thickets to attract Cedar Waxwings, grouse and Mountain Bluebirds, while Wild Rose will provide a thorny defense that attracts finches and sparrows.

__Chipping Sparrows__ feed on the ground, nest in shrubs and sing from the highest trees. Tanagers and grosbeaks sing and feed in the canopy level but nest in the shrubby under-story.

Edges: *Bird variety is greatest where two or more plant communities come together. Shrubby edges are especially important to wild birds because they provide shelter from weather extremes, nesting places, protection from predators such as hawks, and abundant food sources from insects and fruits throughout the year.*
(Kress 1985)

The edges (above) combine water and a hedge line while the pavement edge (right) creates a dense shelter belt to provide privacy and wildlife cover.
Top: Bob Johnson, Right: Gayle Shugars

Group the plants in interesting clusters and spaces while remembering they do grow up and out! Carefully chosen shrub and tree diversity can provide buffers to street noise, desiccating winds and blowing snows, while offering a seasonal display of showy flowers, edible fruit and textured stems and branches. Not only does this provide a variety of types of habitats, but wherever two areas of different vegetation structure meet, you also are creating a new edge - an important zone of greatly increased structural diversity.

Designing Great Edges

Identify every edge in your landscape - where lawn meets pavement, where garden meets lawn, where garden meets house, and where your boundary abuts a neighbor's. Even if you enjoy having a formal garden or a manicured lawn, you can probably also set aside a little corner space that has some wildness about it. Natural habitats aren't orderly and neat, so go beyond stylized order to include eye-appealing curves, leafy shrubs and clumpy tufts that draw your eye and senses into the tumbling tangles and riotous colors. Then watch your wildscape come alive with sunny goldfinches and colorful butterflies.

MEET A HABITAT HERO:
GREAT DIVERSITY AT GLENWOOD SPRINGS

Garfield County - Piñon-Juniper Woodland Jim Knopf

For Sharill, gardening is a passion - "no I think it is an addiction." Their landscape reveals a great diversity of naturalized plants - aspen, cottonwoods, chokecherries and wild roses - and a free-running creek. And the yard is a wildlife mecca with Black Bears, Cutthroat Trout, Beavers, salamanders and many, many birds including a Great Horned Owl, American Kestrel and Great Blue Heron.

DILEMMA: Thistles were everywhere, especially along the creek running through their five-acre property and pasture area. Sharill acquired two goats and two llamas and the problem was solved! All the dandelions really bother her husband; so they eat them, live with them and appreciate them, while their Swiss mountain dog loves the bright yellow flowers so much that he also eats a lot of them - problem almost solved!

PROVIDING DIVERSITY: The chokecherry bushes and wild roses provide essential cover and food. There are several old cottonwoods, spruce and aspens that attract a wide variety of birds. The wooded areas are left undisturbed, along with downed trees and a large brush pile. There are three traditional birdfeeders, one hummingbird feeder, and two dried corncob feeders for the squirrels, chipmunks and jays. No pesticides are used, so there are bugs and critters everywhere. Flowerbeds aren't cut back in the fall, to help provide winter interest, natural protection for the smaller less hardy plants, and seeds and berries for the wildlife.

WILDSCAPING TIP: Managing wildlife mischief is a full-time task here, so they resort to clever strategies such as wrapping chicken wire around young aspens to control the Beaver damage, hanging bird feeders high off the ground to reduce bear problems, and most remarkable, walking the dog around the apple trees, vegetable garden, and flower beds to deter deer. (See Managing Wildlife Mischief on page 48 for more deer deterrents.) Sharill recommends that you enjoy the garden throughout the day and in all seasons, including all the scents and sounds. "Take risks, experiment with new and old plant material and don't get overwhelmed if everything doesn't get planted or maintained right when it's supposed to."

FAVORITE PLANT: All the fruit-bearing plants such as gooseberries, elderberries, currants and apple trees, which they've learned to share with all the wildlife. Their son likes plants that smell lemony, piney and minty.

An uprooted tree trunk provides sculptural elements as well as a perch for foraging song birds. Bob Johnson

Creating Brush Piles

Brush piles also make great perches and provide nooks and crannies to hide in. So don't haul those fallen limbs and pruned twigs to the dump. Instead, take advantage and recycle them into a brush pile that you can build and keep adding to at the edge of your wildscape. Create a foundation from rocks or logs, then place branch stems pointing toward the ground; finish with piling cut shrubs and pruned branches on top. Now you've created a maze of tunnels to provide security from predators and shelter from weather extremes. Wind blown leaf litter will attract sparrows, towhees and thrashers who will hunt for insects among the fallen leaves.

Increasing Nesting Opportunities

The same principles of vertical and horizontal diversity will provide a greater variety of nesting sites for a whole community of bird species. Different birds choose to nest at different levels above the ground - or even on the ground - and in different kinds of vegetation. The evergreens that stand up to the winter winds and protect the birds that cluster in their branches will come alive in the spring with the songs of different species that will raise their young on the same branches.

The Beauty of Dead Trees

If you happen to have a large dead tree - a snag - in your yard, where it does not endanger passers-by or structures, consider yourself fortunate. An old snag is home to many wiggly insects, which makes it a certain magnet for woodpeckers to peck on for food. Dead tree limbs become yard art and active perches for sparrows and finches. If the idea is unsightly to you, plant a vine on the dead tree as a vegetative cover. Choose from Virginia Creeper for great fall color and seeds that attract Downy Woodpeckers, or Sweet Autumn Clematis for a great bird shelter or Twinberry Honeysuckle for moist areas, providing nectar for hummingbirds and fruit for other birds.

Dead trees create an entirely different kind

of nesting opportunity for birds known as cavity nesters such as woodpeckers, which will excavate a cavity in the dead wood to raise their young there. Once the woodpeckers move on, many other species are ready to move in and take advantage of the woodpeckers' handiwork, from wintering flocks of chickadees, Brown Creepers and nuthatches to summering families of Screech Owls.

Dead, dying, hollow trees and fallen logs provide homes for some four hundred species of birds, mammals and amphibians. Of course, if there is a potential for harm, clean up the debris or move it to another, safer garden site.

Adding Nest Boxes to Your Wildscape

As old forests have been cut down and replaced by younger ones, fewer snags remain, making secure nest sites scarce for cavity-nesting birds. Consequently, birdhouses are a beneficial addition to your wildscape. Birdhouses - or nest boxes - come in many shapes and sizes, depending upon the species of bird that you want to attract.

Location, Location, Location is the Key!

The same nest box at different levels on a tree attracts different species; the hole size is species-specific too. If the entry hole is too big, larger birds will rob the nest of its eggs or chicks, or non-native invasive birds like European Starlings or House Sparrows may move in.

Bluebirds like perching on fence posts and prefer open sites bordering open fields and lawns. Chickadees use nest boxes that are in more secluded woody areas. It's important to look for houses that are designed to repel predators and resist destructive weather elements, which sometimes excludes the overly creative hand-made houses. Visit *www.audubon.org* for more details.

Birds, insects and snakes welcomed here - cats beware! Bob Johnson

MEET A HABITAT HERO:
ORGANIC STEWARDSHIP IN MANITOU SPRINGS

Becky feels gardening allows her to live the life that she's here for: to teach, to live in and create beauty. "I can landscape all year round and support myself and my habit of enjoying natural beauty, being in the sunshine, singing and laughing, listening to the birds."

El Paso County - Piñon-Juniper Woodland Bob Johnson

DILEMMA: Dogs and plantings don't always work together but Becky's canine companions are part of her family. She's adapted her yard to minimize the dogs' playful antics by using ornamental wood, rocks and garden novelties to protect her plants from being crushed, creating a very eclectic landscape. Becky's goal is sustainable landscaping that requires little attention: restoration of the soil (after bluegrass), drought water sharing and gray water methods, creating an edible forest garden from scratch.

PROVIDING DIVERSITY: In the foothills at 6,500 feet, year-round wildlife feeding is a commitment reflected in her plant choices: Bee Balm, snapdragons, asters and herbs; berries and seeds from Grape Holly, Nanking Cherry, Cotoneaster and currant; and maple, aspen and elm trees for the insect-eating birds. Light mulches, like straw, break down the soil, providing layers of organic matter for many insects that, in turn, provide food sources for three resident snakes, field mice and a variety of birds. Her habitat focuses mainly on birds and smaller denizens, though she enjoys hearing the coyotes, smelling the foxes and skunks, enjoying the antics of raccoons and cursing the deer.

WILDSCAPING TIP: Becky's landscape is hand-watered infrequently but deeply. Her garden tips include low water usage, Xeriscape sensibility and a non-chemical stance on the land. Her most important tip is on the virtues of patience in landscaping. She feels that so many folks are in a hurry and often times miss the journey of building gardens at a slower pace.

FAVORITE PLANT: As a landscaper, Becky loves "cast-iron" plants that require little water and offer wildlife benefits. Some of her favorites are: Rocky Mountain Penstemon, salvias and sages, chokecherry, junipers and conifers of all varieties.

Providing Food

In addition to shelter and nesting, another essential ingredient of any habitat is a ready supply of food for the animals living there. In your wildscape you'll want to grow a variety of plants that provide different kinds of food at different seasons of the year. In the case of birds, each species tends to specialize in certain kinds of food in a given season - seeds, berries, insects, flower nectar - so you'll want to get familiar with the diets of the birds in your area.

Natural Plantings

Offering specific food for specific species guarantees the best results; and knowing what works in your area is critical. For example, Lesser Goldfinches are present in some areas all summer and fall. In early and mid-summer, they feed on insects along with seeds from Indian Ricegrass, Mexican Hat, and Blanket Flower. By late summer they're eating the perennial Nuttall's Sunflower seeds and clamber all over the seed heads of the annual sunflowers in the fall.

For diversity and interest, include plants with different bloom periods, interesting textures and bold contrasting colors. For instance, most crabapples are non-native, though tough drought-tolerant trees that survive well at elevations as high as 9,000 feet and provide an important food source for Townsend's Solitaires and American Robins. Edible currant or gooseberry species thrive in amended soil but tolerate dry rocky slopes up to 10,000 feet.

Food Availability: Enhanced food supply increases a bird's chances for survival as well as for a more productive breeding season. Available food, both natural and supplemental, determines the male's energy to display and defend his territory and the number of nestlings and juveniles the pair can maintain. Migration also requires extensive energy requirements. With many smaller bird species flying at night, making food available during morning stopovers can contribute significantly to their survival.

Well thought out plant selections provide year-round sources of nectar, fruit and berries for all wildlife. Top: Stephen Jones, Bottom right: Bill Schmoker, Above: City of Boulder OSMP

Insect & Bird Connections

Black-capped Chickadee

White-breasted Nuthatch

Violet-green Swallow

Western Tanager

Flowers provide both nectar and pollen for hummingbirds, butterflies, moths and bees, while other parts of plants provide food in many forms. Western Thimbleberry provides both flowers and edible fruit. Wildlife such as chipmunks and Steller's Jays benefit from seed-producing plants. June brings the red fruits of Saskatoon Serviceberry, fall brings the brilliant foliage and blackish berries of Virginia Creeper, and red chokecherries will likely create feeding frenzies. Gambel's Oak and Ponderosa Pine produce important seed crops for foraging Band-tailed Pigeons, Rock Squirrels, Scrub Jays and nuthatches. Wildlife food requirements are much like our own: variety and constant supply.

Birds Love Insects

Elm, hackberry, willow, aspen, and cottonwoods provide food for wildlife indirectly in the form of the insects they attract. If these trees are healthy and have good growing conditions, they play host to huge and diverse insect populations, which in turn attract diverse populations of insect-eating birds. This is part of nature's balance, in which all parts of the living system are connected; spraying pesticides disrupts that balance by killing the insects and depriving birds of these food supplies.

If a tree has an insect infestation, examine its growing conditions. Insect infestations are simply symptoms, not the cause of the problem. Spraying chemicals is rarely the solution. Spraying will, in fact, kill a lot of desirable insects like moths and butterflies. In the spring, migration is timed exquisitely with unfolding green leaves and spring caterpillars. This is the food of warblers and other migrating insect eaters such as Mountain Bluebirds and Green-tailed Towhees, providing them the energy to continue their travels and set up nesting territories.

Warblers eat insects almost exclusively and can be attracted with a layered vegetative canopy catering to their eating niches and habitat preferences. For instance, Virginia's Warblers favor dense thickets and shrubs in the foothills; Yellow Warblers favor shrublands and groves of aspens, willows and cotton-woods; and Common Yellowthroats favor cattail marshes and wetland brambles. When you create a habitat for these birds, they will repay the favor by helping to control insect populations around your house naturally.

A Mouse-eared Bat house is another insect-control option since this species consumes tremendous quantities of evening-flying insects. If you really feel that you have too many insects around, try attracting Barn Swallows or other swallow species. Barn Swallows can fly six hundred miles each day scooping up insects to feed their broods - a total of 8,000 insects per nest per day! Toxic chemicals are no match for this kind of natural control!

Broad-tailed Hummingbird also eats insects and sips nectar from blooms such as this delphinium.
Lynn & Bruce Bowen

MEET A HABITAT HERO:
HUMMINGBIRD ORCHARD IN CLIFTON

Steve and Debbie plant to provide food and protection for wildlife, to attract hummingbirds and to add beauty and interest to their lives. "Each year we host various groups to our gardens to learn more about planting for wildlife, to watch hummingbirds and our banding activities."

Mesa County - Semi-Desert Shrubland Bob Johnson

DILEMMA: Blending flower and vegetable gardens into the native desert areas has been their greatest challenge. Selecting xeric plants such as Western Chokecherry, Nanking Cherry, Greasewood, and Shadscale, along with dryland grasses such as Side-oats Grama, Indian Ricegrass, Sheep Fescue, and Little Bluestem that need little irrigation, has helped integrate the cultivated areas with the surrounding native landscape.

PROVIDING DIVERSITY: The fruit orchards and vineyards benefit from a nearby irrigation canal and the Colorado River. A wildlife shelterbelt started twenty-five years ago now has over 350 trees and shrubs, varieties selected to provide wildlife cover and food, such as Burr Oak and Rocky Mountain Juniper, Mountain Mahogany, Golden Currant and New Mexico Olive. Piñon Pines attract Scrub Jays and chickadees, while the junipers' prolific berries and cover serve many species including night-roosting Gambel's Quail.

Steve and Debbie's plant selections and feeders attract over 90 bird species, including all four Colorado hummingbirds, while the orchard offers nesting habitat for Black-chinned Hummingbirds. Brush piles constructed from fruit tree pruning provide great cover and insect forage while serving as a magnet for birds, rabbits and Rock Squirrels. American Kestrels, Northern Flickers, and Western Screech-Owls use bird boxes throughout the property. Orioles were observed harvesting and feeding their nestlings from the many caterpillars on a Desert Four-O-Clock - "the best bug control."

WILDSCAPING TIP: "Exclusion and deterrence:" a fifteen-inch-high wire fence keeps rabbits and squirrels out of the flower garden. They are experimenting with red pepper-based sprays to reduce deer damage to trees. Steve and Debbie feel that the most serious challenge to wildscaping and backyard wildlife comes from free-roaming pet and feral cats taking birds. They understand that there is no easy solution but believe more public attention and remedies supported by conservation organizations are needed.

FAVORITE PLANT: Penstemon varieties that attract hummingbirds; Piñon Pine for the Scrub Jays and chickadees; junipers for the berries; buffaloberry since birds love the thorny protection and berries.

Supplemental Feeding

Because it's unlikely that the plants in your wildscape can provide all the food needed by the birds that use the habitat, especially after the summer growing season is over, you may want to put out supplemental food in a bird feeder. Many people do this because they thrill at the sight of the diverse birds that they can attract with different kinds of foods and feeders. But if you're thoughtful in your approach to bird feeding, you can provide a valuable service to the birds while you get to enjoy watching them in your yard.

Over 100 North American bird species supplement their natural food diets with backyard feeding stations. Different birds are attracted to different kinds of seed; look at their bills since the various shapes define the type of seed that birds can eat.

Spring *is a crucial feeding period since most of the natural foods have been consumed over the winter. Supply a diversity of seed to sustain a variety of birds.*

Summer *brings the greatest food requirements since parent birds must not only provide for themselves but their young as well. Though insect populations are at their highest, supplemental feeding is still a great benefit. This is the time to put out sugar water feeders for the hummingbirds and orioles, but take in feeders at night in bear country to avoid habituating bruins and turning them into nuisance bears that are likely to be killed.*

Fall *is another season of great food demand since bird populations are at their highest levels and the rigors of migration are foremost. This is the time when flight and body feathers are replaced, requiring a large amount of protein and energy.*

Winter *supplemental feeding is of the greatest value to all birds. Make seed and suet supplies available at dawn and dusk since these are the major periods in the day for foraging. Birds increase their feeder visits in harsh weather, especially after snowfalls. When natural foods are scarce or inaccessible, small birds like juncos and finches would benefit from having a seed source to help them survive the frigid nights.*

Try offering a variety of food for the greatest diversity of birds:

Bill Schmoker

Black-oil Sunflower:	*small feeder birds such as chickadees and nuthatches*
Striped Sunflower:	*large-beaked birds such as jays and woodpeckers*
White Millet:	*small-beaked ground feeders such as quail and sparrows*
Thistle:	*goldfinches, House Finches and Common Redpolls*
Suet:	*insect-eating birds such as wrens and woodpeckers*
Peanuts:	*woodpeckers, jays, chickadees and titmice*
Amaranthus:	*Red-winged Blackbirds, goldfinches (a single plant can produce over 100,000 tiny seeds!)*
Cosmos:	*Lesser Goldfinches*
Broom corn:	*White-crowned Sparrows*
Purple Coneflowers:	*goldfinches*
Sugar Solution:	*hummingbirds and orioles*
Fruit, raisins:	*American Robins, mockingbirds and nuthatches*

Feeder Locations

Place feeders at different locations: sparrows, juncos and towhees are ground feeders, so supply table-like, wire mesh feeders; finches and chickadees feed in shrubs and trees, so supply tube feeders.

Build a multilevel structure incorporating a covered bird feeder, a convenient perch made from a tree limb and a slippery metal or plastic baffle to ward off raccoons and squirrels.

Place the feeding station facing south and away from our strong northerly winds. More than rain or snow, winds deter birds from feeding to minimize energy loss. Also, keep the ground area free of tall grasses and away from shrubbery to deter prowling cats.

Prevent window collisions by placing feeders within three feet of the windows if possible.

Your consistent feeding will make life easier for many birds, especially during the winter. However, by providing a feeding area, you must also accept that your yard will attract hungry raptors. Hawks, like Sharp-shinned Hawks and Northern Harriers, will commonly capture the older, weaker birds, as well as the unluckier ones. Hawks at least only kill what they need to eat, unlike cats that will kill even if very well fed.

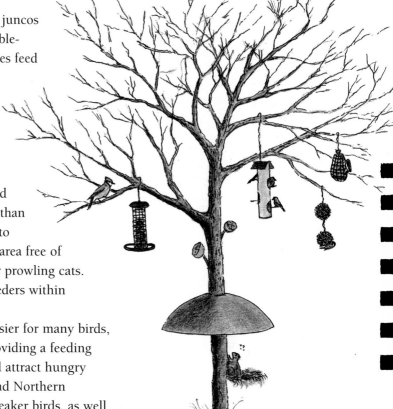

Providing Water

In semi-arid regions like Colorado, water can be even more of a limiting factor in your habitat than food. While birds can obtain much of their water needs from their food, all species need at least some water for both drinking and bathing throughout the year. Small seed-eating birds must drink at least 10 percent of their total body weight in fresh water every day. So providing an accessible supply of water in your wildscape will meet an important need of all your resident birds while also serving as a major attractant for a large variety of visitors.

Bird Baths

A consistent year-round clean water feature such as a simple birdbath can provide window-watching adventures, whereas a sporadic water supply will definitely limit the diversity of wildlife visitors. Lesser Goldfinches and hummingbirds are often attracted to moving and dripping water, including spray from a garden hose.

Songbirds don't swim and most commercial

Water is a magnet for this iridescent Widow Skimmer Dragonfly.
Top: Scott Severs, Bottom: Bob Johnson.

baths are too deep. Add a layer of rocks so the depth doesn't exceed 2 inches, with sloping sides working best. Placement is important since wet birds are easy prey for roaming cats. Place bird baths on a stump rather than directly on the ground, and position them 10 or more feet away from dense vegetation.

Locate birdbaths and feeders in areas that receive morning sun if possible. After a long cold winter night, birds will appreciate morning sun that thaws frozen water as early each day as possible. Change the water every few days to prevent any mold build-up, which can be life threatening to birds.

If you already have an artificial, pre-form pond in your wildscape, capitalize on this focal point by maximizing the habitat benefits of providing water. Planting water plants such as Prairie Cordgrass, sedges and Marsh Milkweed will supply oxygen and provide habitat for all the water creatures including aquatic dragonfly nymphs. Now, install a perch slightly elevated above the water surface so that colorful adult dragonflies can alight!

Wildscape Notes

3

DESIGNING AND BUILDING YOUR WILDSCAPE

Creating a Wildscape Plan

Now it's time to design your own wildscape. Using the plan you drew of the features of your existing site, begin sketching in your proposed changes. (You may want to make several photocopies of the site plan first. Or if you're more comfortable sketching on a computer, use any existing garden or landscape design program.) Draw in planned features such as paths, berms, stream channels, shade structures and others. Sketch in groups of plants and make a master plant list of all the species and varieties you will use.

Think diversity - horizontal, vertical, and diversity of shape, flowering, fruiting, and cover - when choosing plantings, since more kinds of plants and plantings will support more varied species of birds, butterflies and other wildlife. See the suggested native plant selections on page 74.

It's important to group plants of similar water needs together since plants that need less water actually live shorter lives if overwatered. Also keep in mind the layout of existing irrigation systems and the location of existing hose connections.

In terms of design, it's all up to you. Do you want your wildscape to look informal and colorful, whimsical and wild, rustic and woodsy, or more formal and disciplined? Wildscapes can suit any or all of those tastes. Now it's time to design a personal wildscape that beckons you outside, captivates your senses and gladdens your spirit — it's all about finding joy in Nature!

1 HUMMINGBIRD/BUTTERFLY GARDEN
(WILD/XERISCAPE PERENNIALS)
2 MIXED-BUNCHGRASS PRAIRIE
3 LOW BERM WITH NATIVE AND XERISCAPE SHRUBS
AND PERENNIAL WILDFLOWERS
4 NATIVE GRASS "LAWN" WITH WILDFLOWERS
5 DWARF TALL FESCUE MIX LAWN
6 MOUNTAIN SHRUBLAND UNDERPLANTED WITH
PERENNIAL WILDFLOWERS
7 ROCK GARDEN
FLAGSTONES OR PAVERS
ELEVATED BIRDBATH

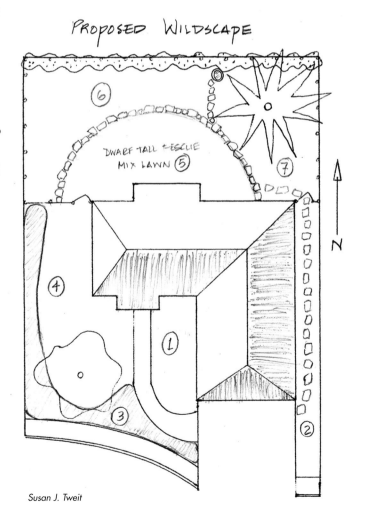

PROPOSED WILDSCAPE

DWARF TALL FESCUE MIX LAWN ⑤

N

Susan J. Tweit

With bluegrass removed, the Plains wildscape (below) now attracts Bullock's Orioles and Rufous Hummingbirds while Buffalograss and Plains Yucca (left) thrive in the right location.
Left: David Winger
Below: Bob Johnson

Going Beyond Lawns

As Wallace Stegner poetically stated in an essay in *Where the Bluebird Sings to the Lemonade Springs*, we "have to get over the color green…". Here in Colorado, that means getting over our obsession with lawns brought from wetter climates. In our semi-arid conditions, Kentucky Bluegrass and other high-water lawns require lots of fertilizer and pesticides to look good plus gulp huge amounts of our finite water supply. A one-acre lawn in Longmont, for example, required 75,000 gallons during the hotter summer months to stay green - that's a lot of drinking water!

You can shrink your lawn, your water bill, and your time spent maintaining your landscaping, and increase your pleasure in your yard, by converting to waterwise wildscaping plantings. That Longmont landscape, for instance, is evolving into a wildscape by incorporating new berms planted with native shrubs and wildflowers, and replacing the old Kentucky Bluegrass with Enviroturf® (a mix of Tall Fescue, Smooth Brome, and Canada Bluegrass) that uses 30 to 40% less water.

You can keep a lawn and still save water by planting native grasses like Buffalograss or Blue Grama. Buffalograss is ideally suited for clay soils in hot, sunny locations up to 7,000 feet elevation, but not for sandy or rich soils. The two most-commonly used varieties of Buffalograss are Legacy®, which greens up sooner in spring but also browns off earlier in fall, and 609®, which stays green later in fall and is slower to green up in spring. Legacy® is available in all-female cultivars, which don't produce pollen (lawn grass pollen is a major contributor to rising respiratory allergy rates in urban areas). Buffalograss can be grown from seed but is easier to establish with sod or plugs.

Blue Grama, a native bunchgrass with somewhat longer, fine-textured leaves, is ideal for water-saving lawns at higher elevations and in cooler areas, or areas with well-drained soil. It can also be mixed with Buffalograss for a contrast in texture and color.

Buffalograss and Blue Grama lawns are lovely with an under-planting of naturalizing bulbs, like species tulips, daffodils, and crocus. These come up before the native grasses green up, bloom, and die back before either lawn needs mowing, thus providing color (and food for early-flying insects) when the lawns are still dormant.

Creating a Pocket Garden

Consider reducing the area of your lawn by creating a pocket garden by replacing a small portion of lawn (maybe under a tree) with showy perennials. Try these plant selections: Pineleaf Penstemon which grows compactly to about one foot tall and has bright red flowers; inter-planted with Shasta Sulfur Buckwheat which has oval blue-green basal leaves and bright yellow blooms. Kansas Gayfeather, with magenta flower spikes in late summer and fall, inter-planted with bright orange Butterflyweed and clumps of Silver Mound Sage. Include fragrant foliage and sunset-pink fall flower spikes of Hummingbird Mint mixed with spring-blooming, yellow-flowered Prince's Plume, and the blue spires of Rocky Mountain Penstemon.

You'll have a season-long show that attracts butterflies and hummingbirds, with little maintenance and not much water required. Or consider a small night garden with blooms like Evening Primrose, Sacred Datura, and Moonflowers. Evening blooms employ moon-bright blossoms and sensuous fragrances to lure nocturnal pollinators like the hawk moth, often taken for a plump, furry-bodied hummingbird. Or plant a fragrance garden and include artemisias, creeping thyme and lavenders.

Pocket Garden with Rabbitbrush, Fernbush, sedums and a dwarf Colorado Blue Spruce. Connie Holsinger

Creating A Wildflower Meadow

If you have open grasslands or a mountain meadow, try your hand at restoring the area with colorful wildflowers reminiscent of Colorado's native heritage. Many mixes include annuals that are self-sowing for first year color, mixed with longer-lasting perennials. Look for Colorado regional mixes that include Blue Flax, Rocky Mountain Beeplant, Desert Marigold and Black-eyed Susan. Be sure to read the seed content and avoid buying mixes that include invasive, non-native plants (see page 47).

Wildscaping on the Patio

If you live in a condo with a balcony, don't despair. Container gardening, along with hanging a tube seed feeder and hummingbird feeder, are the answers to attracting birds and butterflies. Based on the amount of sunlight, choose from grasses as well as continuously blooming annuals such as verbena and salvias. Use moisture-conserving plastic containers or line your clay containers with bubble wrap to preserve moisture, and remember to water as needed. A plant saucer filled with pebbles and water can provide a drinking station as well.

Replacing Lawn

When you're wildscaping an existing yard, you'll probably be replacing lawn. You can start small, by simply extending existing flowerbeds and making new beds around the bases of shrubs and shade trees, or you can convert the whole yard at once.

Either way, you'll need to remove turf wherever you want the wildscape. You can rent a turf-scalper if you want to use the living grass somewhere else, or let the grass die and leave it in place as organic mulch and cut planting holes through it.

Removing the grass doesn't have to involve the use of herbicide. You can actively eliminate the grass by rototilling it or by hand-tilling it with a spade. You'll have to repeat the process at least once, a week or so later, to eliminate any new grass and weed seed sprouts. You can also cover the turf with a layer of newspapers thick enough to block out the sunlight, as our Denver Habitat Hero proved (page 34). However, this does not work on thick spreading turf grass - it grows through the newspaper as the blanket cover disintegrates. (Using carpet and other permeable man-made materials gradually poisons the soil, as toxic glues and other chemicals leach out.) Smothering the grass with sheets of black plastic or other impermeable material is not recommended because it doesn't allow water

Grassless landscapes allow lots of visual interest with waterwise blooms such as penstemon, salvia, yarrow, artemisias and Lamb's Ear. Bob Johnson

through and the heat can build up under the plastic to the point where it kills everything in the surface soil, including other plant roots and insects and microorganisms that make the soil fertile.

Once you've eliminated the lawn in the area of your new wildscape, you're ready to plant! In fact, you need to plant the entire area where you've removed the grass to prevent soil erosion by strong winds or heavy rains. If the ground remains bare for long, you might also have trouble controlling the weeds that will quickly move into the cleared area. This is why you may want to take on the conversion of only a small area of lawn at any one time.

Meet a Habitat Hero:
A Gated Wildscape in Denver

B arbara's goal was to create a yard that would be a park-like peaceful oasis to block out the city chaos. "It's an incredible world out there, and everything has a purpose. I consider it a gift to have a dragonfly visit my yard!"

Denver County - Plains Grassland Connie Holsinger

DILEMMA: Buying a city-size lot in Denver brought many gardening challenges for Barbara. Along with many diseased trees and shrubs, bluegrass was everywhere and "a huge hassle to keep green, mowed and weed-free." Little by little, Barbara's hands-on efforts have eliminated all the bluegrass. Her technique involved covering the grass with a layer of newspaper 12 sheets thick and saturating this layer with water. Then the layers were covered with 350 bags of soil, which she bought on sale and hauled into the yard one at a time. This backyard now meanders through flagstone pathways, raised planting beds, a cedar deck enveloping a huge Silver Maple and an untamed corner that hosts a lot of wildness!

PROVIDING DIVERSITY: Plantings include berry-producing shrubs and trees to feed wildlife and provide fall colors, such as Pin Oak and hawthorns, Cotoneasters and chokecherries and serviceberry. Combinations of flowers and vines attract hummingbirds, bees and butterflies, while overhanging branches support oodles of zany birdhouses and feeders. A cedar fence encloses the entire lot "to provide a sense of privacy and tranquility...I love watching all the life and activities going on among the birds, butterflies, moths, bees, spiders, and lady bugs." Barbara even invites the squirrels in by simply adding another feeder - up to nine now! Her main source of pleasure is feeding the birds year-round and listening to their sounds through the day. "Absolutely delightful!"

WILDSCAPING TIP: Always adding mulch and compost - "I should have a mountain in the backyard but I don't".

FAVORITE PLANT: Barbara loves all the berry-producing bushes, along with Catmint, Wine Cups, ornamental grasses, and asters.

Creating a Waterwise Wildscape

Consider that 50% of the water used annually by the average household on the Front Range, where most of Colorado's population is concentrated, is used for landscaping! This represents an enormous opportunity to reduce our demand for our finite supplies of water by redesigning our landscapes to follow waterwise and Xeriscape principles, which are integral to wildscaping in Colorado.

Not only does waterwise wildscaping help protect our drinking water supplies, but it benefits wildlife all over Colorado as well. Every living creature in our state depends for survival on the same rainfall and snowfall that is the source of all the water we need and use in our homes and businesses. As our statewide population keeps growing, our total water consumption will surely grow, resulting in reduced river flows, degraded riparian and wetland habitats, and less water generally to meet all the needs of our fish and wildlife. But imagine, instead, how we could offset that potential damage by converting the average home's landscape to a waterwise wildscape. And the reduction in water use and maintenance will save you money, too!

As you implement your wildscape design, try to incorporate as many of the following waterwise fundamentals as possible to reduce your dependence on supplemental irrigation, improve water quality around your home and cut your maintenance costs:

Top, Swamp Milkweed. Above, One-sided Penstemon. Stephen Jones

🐦 **Plan wisely for the environmental conditions of your property.**

Plant low-water use plants in areas with dryer conditions such as sunny, south-facing slopes and exposure to winds. Plant any higher-water use plants only in wetter areas or areas that are shaded and protected from the wind. A well-placed tree or hedge can help reduce desiccating winds.

🐦 **Choose native plants whenever possible.**

Native plants are well adapted to Colorado's environmental conditions and can survive on natural precipitation. See page 38 for more information on transitioning to native plants and page 74 for a list of wildlife friendly native selections.

Group plants with similar water needs together.

This is one of the most important things you can do to create a truly waterwise wildscape. If plants with different water needs are mixed, you will tend to water enough to satisfy the thirstiest plants, and this will waste water on the plants that need less. If you want to include some plants in your design that require more water, at least keep them together in just one part of the wildscape and zone the irrigation accordingly.

Create waterwise lawn areas.

Most lawns require higher amounts of watering, so you can save water by reducing the size of any lawn areas and choosing low water-use grasses. See Going Beyond Lawns on page 31.

Water wisely.

Water only when absolutely necessary, and then do so in the early morning or late evening when it's cooler, to minimize evaporation. Also avoid using fine-spray sprinklers to reduce evaporation losses. Drip irrigation and soaker hoses used for shrubs and trees in wildscaping are far more water efficient. Your goal should be to water less frequently but at deeper levels, giving roots the moisture they need to grow. In the winter, when root growth is continuing, you may need to water occasionally if there's little snow or rain. The Habitat Hero from Manitou Springs feels that deeper roots are the best defense against water shortages. She says that by watering deeper and less frequently, "my garden may not be glistening with fat and sassy, well-watered plants, but my gardens are indeed hardy, with sturdy, healthy plants."

Waterwise plants such as (opposite page) Coreopsis, Poppy Mallow, Purple Coneflower, (right) Dotted Gayfeather, Mexican Hat, and Plains Yucca thrive in water-wise landscapes. David Winger

Consider mulches.

A layer of mulch on the soil surface can help preserve soil moisture. The same Manitou Springs gardener claims she's "a mulching fool since mulching the soil to withstand more heat and require less water...brings her root insurance". But beware of heavy mulching around low-water use plants, which require dry soil much of the time. Too much mulch can keep the soil too wet for too long. See page 42 for more information on mulching.

Protect water quality.

You can prevent run-off of silt and chemicals from your yard into nearby streams, or leaching into the groundwater, by avoiding over-watering and over-fertilizing, reducing your use of pesticides, and covering any bare soil areas with plants or mulch.

For additional information and extensive web-based links to Xeriscape and Water-Smart Gardening information, visit these web sites: Denver Water at *www.denverwater.org*; Denver Botanic Gardens at *www.botanicgardens.org*; and Green Industries of Colorado (an alliance of plant and landscape trade associations) at *www.greenco.org*.

Selecting Plants: Going Native

Consider replacing your high-water plants with a selection of low-water users and natives since water can be a scarce resource in Colorado. If snowfall falls short, our reservoirs are low and the water we use for irrigation diminishes Colorado's rivers as well as our drinking water supply even further. Since native plants are adapted to our climate, they tend to need less water once they're established and they do well in our soils. They're also more readily recognizable to our native wildlife as sources of food. And developing a healthy wildscape of native plants is an important contribution to our efforts to rid the natural landscape of exotic invasives that threaten the vitality and carrying capacity of wildlife habitats.

Think about transitioning to natives over several growing seasons as you become familiar with what's available and what does well in your own wildscape region. Visit local nature centers, Xeriscape

Broad-tailed Hummingbird on Indian Paintbrush. ©Wendy Shattil/Bob Rozinski
Top Right: Golden Banner, Trailing Fleabane, Bell's Twinpod. Dave Sutherland
Below: Golden Aster, Spotted Gayfeather, Blue Campanula. Dave Sutherland

Blue Mist Penstemon.
Dave Sutherland
Mountain Ash.
City of Boulder OSMP

demonstration gardens and the Denver Botanic Gardens. Check out the regional nursery list on page 84 that feature native plants and waterwise selections. Wait for fall nursery sales so you get more plants for your dollars, then select plants of varying growth habits and sizes that will sustain the broadest range of creatures. See page 74 for recommended regional native plant selections.

The following suggestions will help you get started. Get to know the native plants in your region. Take a walk along hiking trails and see native plants in their habitat. Mimic natural communities in what and how you plant. Create planting structures by using windbreaks and raised berms, boulders and arbors.

Choose a site within your existing landscape that can host native plants. If you have lots of shade, consider a woodland garden and plant Colorado Columbine where the soil is dampish. If you have lots of sun, try a butterfly garden and plant Butterflyweed, Rocky Mountain Bee Plant, and Desert Four O'clock to attract sphinx moths in the early evening. If you have a wet area, create a wetland and watch the toads and dragonflies move in; attract nectar- seeking bees with spikes of Fireweed.

Select the plants according to the wildlife you want to attract. Fall bird migration coincides with the fruiting of over 70 percent of bird-distributed plants. Chickadees, grosbeaks and flickers will readily visit patches of Silver Buffaloberry, fruit-bearing viburnums, and Rocky Mountain Juniper. Towhees will scratch under these plants for fallen fruits and berries. The key is to provide year-round food sources. Match your plant selection to the soil: Black-eyed Susan and Blanket Flower for dry sites, and Tall Beard Tongue with its bluish blooms for less dry locations.

MEET A HABITAT HERO:
NATIVE WILDSCAPING IN NORTH BOULDER

Boulder County - Plains Grassland Bob Johnson

Dave feels that "gardening is special. It's like painting, but with living things...constantly changing with the seasons, a microcosm of small ecological stories going on under our noses and daring us to notice!" He considers the garden as a teaching work in progress: "I have learned a great deal about native plants and am now competent to lead wildflower identification walks and host native plant gardening programs."

DILEMMA: Conforming to city code, a fencing project to screen out traffic noise created a "long stupid-looking strip of parched lawn along the sidewalk." Not to be undone, Dave brought in boulders, xeric native shrubs and native trees. A busy pedestrian sidewalk became a classroom when he marked all the native plants with metal signs: "it's a little botany lesson and helps promote native gardening."

PROVIDING DIVERSITY: A birdbath dish provides year-round water while the garden itself is a big wildlife feeder, especially when Mule deer visit. Tiger Swallowtails can be seen on the chokecherry while the white blossoms of the Stemless Evening Primroses are visited by the White-lined Sphinx Moths at dusk. Painted Lady butterflies enjoy the fall blooms of rabbitbrush. The huge yellow flowers from a patch of prickly pear cacti attract bees and pollinating beetles. Milkweeds attract a whole community of nectaring insects and symbiotic invertebrates, while aphids attract lacewing larvae and Lady Bird beetles.

WILDSCAPING TIP: Dave never uses insecticides since "insects are half the show!" Mule Deer bucks savaged some tree trunks and shrubs with their antlers, so he wraps deer netting around all the small vegetation in the fall. "I have tried to accept the deer damage as one of the consequences of a wildlife-friendly garden...but my resolve was severely tested this year when they bit off all my treasured Shooting Star flowers just before they bloomed."

FAVORITE PLANT: He loves the native penstemons for their exuberant and colorful flowers and for being so forgiving when transplanted. "I love a clump of native Wild Iris planted by a downspout and wait for it to bloom every year - a real treasure."

Moving the Dirt and Planting the Seeds

Getting Started

Once you've decided to change your landscape into a wildscape, the next step is to transfer your plans to the ground. You can draw your new plantings and other wildscaping features by outlining them with string, stakes or a garden hose laid on the ground, or by using a non-toxic spray paint to sketch the outlines directly on the soil.

These methods allow you to see the outlines of your wildscape before you break ground. Take time to look at your outlines from all angles, from inside and outside your house, and make sure that you like what you see before you start wildscaping.

Now you can start building and placing the major features: set boulders, and do any excavation and construction. Build mounds, terraces, structures, patios, water features, and walks before you plant. At higher elevations, rock walls and fences are important buffers in moderating weather extremes and lengthening the growing season.

Next you can start thinking about bringing in the plants. But remember that the timing of Colorado's growing season is varied, with the season in the Front Range beginning in earnest in

Adding structural features: the raised mound (above) hosts yuccas, sundrops and poppies; the rock garden (below) caters to hummingbirds and bees. Top: Panayoti Kelaidis, Below: Bob Johnson.

May for tender annuals and perennials, though bare root stock can be planted as early as March if the soil has warmed up. The Western Slope growing season starts in April in most areas, while the foothills to the higher mountain elevations vary greatly with the highest areas blooming as late as June. Most nursery stock is grown below 6000 feet, so plants destined for higher elevations will probably need to be slowly acclimated to mountain conditions over a period of days or weeks. Talk with your local nursery to determine when it's safe to put out your new plants. Colorado gardeners know it's risky business to plant early but often get fooled by our warming sunshine and cloudless skies.

Buying and Placement of Plants

After you've put the major features in place, it's time to buy plants and arrange them. Make a plant list, including species names, and decide how many and what size of each you'll need. If you're planning large areas of native grassland or meadow, it's less expensive to start from seeds. See Resources on page 84 for nurseries specializing in native and wildscaping plants, or order plants and seeds by mail or on the Internet.

Place your plants roughly where your plans indicate, but don't plant them. Stand back and look at the arrangements; walk around them; go inside your house and look out the windows to make sure their placement is pleasing and not blocking views or creating other problems. Remember that plants grow, so visualize what they'll look like in a few years and allow plenty of space for them to expand upwards and outwards. If the layout looks good, then you're ready to plant!

Dig your holes wider than deep, and break up root balls that are tight or pot-bound (soaking them in water first often makes this easier). Water each hole and let the water sink into the soil so that your new plant starts out with a moist environment. Make a low mound of native soil in the bottom of the hole to set the root ball on, and gently spread the roots out over the mound. Then cover the roots with layers of soil. Finally, press down on the soil to remove air pockets and soak the root area.

Mulching: For all but the coolest and wettest soils, mulching the surface is critical to establishing and maintaining healthy plants here in Colorado. With our dramatically fluctuating weather and extremes in elevation, growing plants are in for a roller coaster ride in temperature and moisture extremes. Soil is markedly cooler under a cover of mulch, which also can work wonders in preventing moisture loss and suppressing weeds. Mulch is beneficial, too, for birds and insects since it supports the tiny lives - soil flora and fauna - that towhees, flickers and other litter-foraging birds live on.

As it decays, organic mulch can help enrich the soil with added nutrients and improved moisture retention. It's important to remember, however, that changing your soil in this way is not always beneficial to the native plants of your region. Native plants adapted to dry mineral soils flourish in those soils and not in enriched soils. Non-native plants that prefer more organic soil should be grouped together in one part of your wildscape.

Use plenty of mulch on top of the soil of the new plantings, whether rock or organic mulch like pine bark or needles, chippings, or aged leaves and grass clippings. Keep mulch several inches away from the stems of perennial plants to avoid bark and crown rot. With most mulch, more is not better, with 3 inches being a good depth. Using mulches like redwood or cedar can introduce fungi and other micro-lives that can potentially create garden problems, so consider using aspen chip mulch. If you're allergy-prone from the fungi in organic mulches, use rock mulch (crushed gravel, rounded or pea gravel). Rock mulch doesn't decay and doesn't blow away but also doesn't add any nutrients to the soil, so a yearly addition of manure may be necessary in areas that are not planted with natives.

Wildscaping a New Home

Starting from scratch is both easier and harder than wildscaping an existing yard. It allows you to plan and plant your entire wildscape at once, without having to consider existing vegetation (unless your new lot comes with trees or wild areas that you want to save, in which case you have a head start). Starting from scratch can be daunting, but many builders work with landscapers; some green builders even have lists of native or Xeriscape plants that you can use to wildscape your property at no extra cost. If doing a whole yard yourself seems like too big a task, work with a professional or do one manageably sized area at a time.

If you're starting small and just converting a few corners of your yard, it makes more sense to do it yourself. You'll learn a lot and the experience will be useful when you decide to enlarge your project. If you're starting from scratch or re-wilding an entire yard, calling in an expert makes more sense, although it'll cost you significantly more to hire a landscaper, since you'll be paying their design fee plus labor for installation, in addition to the cost of plant material and any construction materials.

If you're in a hurry and the project is large or complex, hiring a professional can be a good idea. Look for someone who has experience with native plants and wildscaping. Visit their landscaping projects, talk with their clients, and above all, walk your yard with them and see how they respond to your ideas.

If you're a hands-on person who derives a great deal of pleasure from design and planting, it makes sense to do at least part of the project yourself. You can hire a professional for consultation or for the parts of the job that you don't feel comfortable with - design, for instance, or construction, or certain parts of the installation.

A final thought to keep in mind...so many folks are in a hurry and often times miss the journey of building gardens at a slower pace. Gardens are created over a period of time; insect predators show up AFTER the initial pests do; flowers are fleeting but plant foliage and form can be equally beautiful if one slows down to enjoy. The garden's beauty lies in emulating nature's ecosystems, discovering new life there and in the revealing of the mysteries of life itself. (Habitat Hero, Manitou Springs)

4

MAINTAINING YOUR WILDSCAPE

In the past, humans didn't have the kinds of chemical pesticides we often use today to control animals that we considered pests, so instead we outsmarted them. According to Emily Green, as quoted in the Daily Camera (6/11/04), "We'd avoid mosquitoes by clearing stagnant water or stocking ponds with fish that ate them. We'd aerate shrubs to avoid fungus. We'd compost yard clippings killing off weed seeds. We'd stop pruning in the spring to encourage nesting birds who glean aphids. Birds would also get help from lacewings and wasps and ladybugs. Now we've gone from gardening with our wits to using chemicals."

Adopting Healthy Wildscapes

The first and best defense in minimizing pest and weed issues is to start with vibrant, healthy trees and plants. Whenever possible, choose strong native varieties over high-maintenance exotics. If you choose to use synthetic pesticides, even though we don't advocate doing so, please read the label. Not all chemicals are created equal. Avoid those that kill a broad range of insects, such as organophosphate insecticides (Diazinon® is one trade name). Pick the insecticide most specific to your target species. Wherever possible, use less toxic products such as synthetic pyrethroids.

The sign says it all - using pesticides can be unhealthy to humans and wildlife.

Integrated Pest Management

Integrated Pest Management (IPM) provides a proven alternative to using synthetic pesticides. IPM is based on three principles: monitor the pest problem, determine tolerable amounts of insect damage - a few holes in leaves may not be a problem - and apply appropriate and least-harmful strategies and tactics. With IPM, you'll apply only the necessary controls and only when they are needed to handle pests that go beyond a nuisance or unsightly level. Nature isn't some perfect, manicured backdrop - it's a living system that operates on innumerable relationships in balance.

- Go lightly: try nontoxic methods first. For instance, aphids can often be controlled by vigorously hosing down your plants for three days in a row. Infestations of bagworms or tent caterpillars in trees may look horrific but they seldom do serious damage. Prune out the branches with the webs and you'll have greener, thicker foliage next year. Pull weeds when they're small, and mulch thoroughly to prevent their seeds from germinating.

- If non-toxic methods aren't successful, try a biological control or bio-pesticide. Lacewings and ladybugs, for example, prey on soft-bodied insects such as aphids, mealybugs, thrips, mites and scales. Bacillus thuringiensis (Bt), a bacterium, controls many common caterpillar pests and other insect larvae. Several varieties are species-specific, which is preferable. Remember that caterpillars are butterfly larvae, so Bt can also kill butterflies.

- Spray undiluted vinegar on weeds instead of synthetic herbicides. Be sure to coat all plant surfaces thoroughly; you may need to apply vinegar more than once. Two organic products are now available at local garden centers; both are non-selective, won't harm soil microbes and have no long-term residues.

- Know your enemies: Buy a good field guide to insects and a guide to weeds. Not everything is a pest.

- Practice tolerance: A natural yard is a living ecosystem with an abundant variety of pests, predators, volunteer plants and favorite plant species. The much-maligned dandelion provides food for tiny parasitic wasps that attack garden pests. Many pests are dinner for birds: aphid eggs sustain chickadees in winter; Baltimore Orioles dine on tent caterpillars, gulping up to 17 a minute.

- If you must use insecticides, apply them after sundown when bees and butterflies are inactive and in still air to limit drift; resist spraying when plants are in full bloom. Use sprays rather than granules, which wildlife may eat. Know when weeds, pests, and diseases are most vulnerable.

- For more on healthy gardens, go to Audubon At Home at National Audubon's web site *www.audubon.org*.

Recognizing Beneficial Relationships

Especially when it comes to insects, we're too often blind to their benefits and instead assume that they are simply pests damaging our plants or otherwise up to no good. But the vast majority of insects in our wildscapes are beneficial in their relationships to plants or in the services they perform in our yards. Even in the case of insects that can be truly damaging to our plantings, there is often another insect - or a bird or a bat - that is ready to solve the problem if we'll simply get out of its way.

A Niwot beekeeper tending his million honeybees.
Bob Johnson

Wildscaping Sustains a Front Range Beekeeper

Honeybees arrived in North America around 1600 with the first European settlers. The Great Plains formed a natural barrier to westward honeybee migration until gold miners-turned-farmers imported honeybees. By the late 1800s, the Front Range was a center of honey production and the Denver Post enthusiastically reported, "Colorado honey from the irrigated alfalfa makes the purest and best honey in the world." The 1900s brought challenges: urbanization, habitat fragmentation, the gradual decline of feral colonies of honeybees, and finally deadly invasive species - two non-native kinds of parasitic mite - which killed up to 90 percent of the feral colonies of honeybees and more than half of domestic colonies.

Still, one Niwot beekeeper manages to sustain about one million honeybees. Tom feels wildscaping will be critical to maintaining Front Range honeybee habitat. His advice to home gardeners: plant trees such as crabapples, hawthorns, and edible fruit trees for spring blossoms, and summer flowers in shades of blue, violet, pink or yellow that honeybees recognize. And of course, avoid insecticides wherever possible.

More Reasons Not to Use Insecticides

House Wrens: these endearing, tiny creatures can really be aggressive when it comes to opportunistic feeding. When Saw Fly worms attacked a pear tree in a Boulder backyard, two tiny wrens feasted on the worms, eliminating all of them in just two days.

A Boulder gardener has a patch of prickly pear cacti, the thorns causing him great pain, but the huge yellow flowers attract bees and pollinating beetles. Also, the stamens squirm when you insert a finger into the flower, a sure kid pleasure every time.

Successful gardeners and birders are always eager to share their experiences on how they bested, naturally, the wild invaders. Beneficial relationships have a place in your wildscape and there are fabulous resources waiting to help you.

46

Managing Weeds

Be persistent, know your weeds and understand their lifestyle. Annuals live only one growing season and thus put all their energy into producing tons of seeds; perennials persist for years and put more energy into roots.

To eliminate annuals, getting rid of the seed source is key: learn to recognize them when they are still small and pull, rototill, or smother them with layers of cardboard or newspaper before they set seed. Weeding eventually controls even the most persistent annuals if you do not allow them to seed; year after year of pulling the sprouts will exhaust the seed source in the soil. Do not compost annuals bearing seeds - most compost pile temperatures are not hot enough to kill the seeds. Bag them and send them to the dump.

Controlling perennial weeds involves destroying the root, either by judicious use of a dandelion digger (if the plant is small and doesn't spread by rhizomes, horizontal roots) or by use of herbicides for larger plants or those that sprout from the rhizomes. Thoroughly spray the leaves and stems of actively growing plants with undiluted vinegar or vinegar-based herbicides.

A weed, in common usage, is simply a plant out of place, but ecologically, a weed is an invasive non-native species with the potential to crowd out native plants and sever the relationships between plants, insects, other invertebrates, birds and animals that make ecosystems whole and healthy.

Invasive Plant Species

Many introduced plants stay in place and do not take over, thus pose no real threat to the natural habitat - cultivated corn and rice, garden tulips and peonies fall into this innocuous group, for instance. Unfortunately, others are not so well behaved: over 5000 introduced plants currently threaten natural areas and native vegetation in North America. No habitat, including wetlands and grasslands, is safe from these invaders that are displacing and out-competing native plants.

Invasive plant species are estimated to cost millions of dollars per year in damage to crops and wild landscapes; in some cases they have led to the local extinction of wildlife. Controlling the spread of invasive species is one of the critical environmental problems today, and one where each of us can help. Learn the invasive weeds that are a problem in your area and do not purchase these species or plant them, and eradicate them in your landscape. For specific landscape plants to avoid and the native alternatives to consider, visit the Colorado Native Plant Society web site *www.cnps.org*; for more extensive data on invasive weeds, visit The Nature Conservancy's web site *http://tncweeds.ucdavis.edu* and Colorado's Department of Agriculture's noxious weed web site at *www.ag.state.co.us*.

Managing Wildlife Mischief

Mischief management can be the most engaging and humbling of all our wildscaping learning opportunities. Be creative and be persistent. You will win for a while, but never forever! Remember that your wildscape is a habitat that's open to all wildlife, even those that you consider a nuisance. So it may be best to begin by practicing tolerance and trying to live with even the uninvited guests. Maybe the mischief isn't really so bad. But if it is, these Top Tips come from many sources. Some seem silly, some are definitely serious.

Ants

- Sprinkle natural-grade diatomaceous earth in hiding places and entry points.
- Sprinkle fresh mint leaves at entry points. Ants won't crawl over the fragrant leaves.

Aphids

- Use a lint roller to remove from stems and leaves.
- Apply an insecticidal soap.
- Spray with a strong jet of water to wash them off the plant.

Bears

- Keep all trash and garbage in enclosed, secured, metal containers.
- Bring in all hummingbird and birdseed feeders at night.
- Leave nothing outside that can be a food source.

Cats

- Scatter lemon and other citrus peels; cats generally don't like these scents.
- Some cats don't like garden rue.
- Erect a cat run for your cat - a totally enclosed outdoor space (like a dog run).

Deer & Elk

- Protect individual plants with fencing or cages. Simple 7-foot-tall electric fences are nearly fool proof, though some deer will brave the shocks to get apples.
- Placing bird netting or fishing line over the plants may work.
- Plant lists are typically disappointing. Deer do love tulips, laurel, forsythia, crocus and pansies. Deer do not eat daffodils, ignore coral-bells and stay away from highly scented plants such as lavenders, mints and hummingbird mints. Once deer have found a food source, it's extremely difficult to deter them, so be vigilant!
- Apply predator urine, available through many garden catalogs. Meat eaters produce sulfur compounds in the urine, the universal warning sign for prey species.
- Check out sulfur scent based repellents: these work like predator urine, but last up to four months, rain or shine.

- Over-watering of any native or Xeriscape plants will turn them into deer magnets (deer can actually smell the difference between heavily-watered and fertilized plants and those left to grow on their own). However, when these same plants are grown in native soil with only natural precipitation, the deer browsing often drops dramatically.
- Covering areas around desirable plants with cobbles, large rounded rocks, placed close together, makes for unstable footing. Deer and elk avoid areas where footing is not stable.

Gophers & Moles

- Place mothballs in an open top container, then into the hole and don't forget to remove.
- Castor Bean Plants and Tansy, either growing or dried.
- Hot peppers stuffed into holes.

Lawn Grubs

- Turf-type Tall Fescue: It's toxic to grubs.
- Apply corn gluten meal to turf grass in early spring and fall to prevent germination of dandelions and other common weeds.

Rabbits

- Epson salts: sprinkle around plants and hope for the best.
- Foxes and Coyotes can be very effective predators and they have to eat, too!
- Erect a 2- to 3-foot high chicken wire fence buried 12 inches deep with a bend at the bottom.

Raccoons

- Rummaging raccoons can be both appealing and appalling. They can't jump but they can climb. You can enjoy their antics or try to outwit them.
- Conical metal baffles actually do work when hung below bird feeders.
- Use metal garbage/storage cans that can't be chewed through.

Slugs

- Cayenne flakes: very effective, even after rain.
- Bait slugs with a beer or yeast solution in a saucer buried flush with the soil surface.
- Ducks are to slugs as cats are to mice.
- Iron phosphate works wonders, and it's safe.

Squirrels

- Check out sulfur scent repellent - reported to keep squirrels off bird feeders.
- Cayenne pepper: Try mixing it in the birdseed. (It won't hurt the birds.)
- Visit your local bird store to learn the latest in outwitting these wily creatures; baffles will work as long as you position them correctly.
- Marvel at their ingenuity in getting to the seeds, no matter what we do.

Bill Schmoker

Woodpeckers

■ Commercial taste repellents - reported to discourage Flickers from pecking holes in wood siding.

■ Plastic bird netting: worth trying as a temporary repellent. Hang from cup hooks.

■ Plastic owl decoys by themselves aren't very effective; try affixing feathers to the owl to flutter in the wind.

Disclaimer: Keep in mind that wildlife is wild, spunky and hungry so these Top Tips do not come with guarantees. Let us know what really works or doesn't: Contact us by email *aahcolorado@audubon.org*.

Wildscape Notes

MEET A HABITAT HERO:
GETTING ALONG WITH WILD TURKEYS IN BASALT

Pitkin County - Piñon-Juniper Woodland Gayle Shugars

At 6700 feet, Gayle resides in the foothills of an ecotone - where two regions, Pinon-Juniper Woodland and Montane begin to merge. Gayle tells us that she has four birdbaths around her property. "I get the greatest pleasure from watching the birds drink and bathe." She says that gardening is extremely gratifying - we nurture our gardens, and in turn we are nurtured by our gardens.

DILEMMA: The house and gardens are situated below an upslope area that borders the street. The slope is planted with raspberries and perennials, while at street level native shrubs such as Big Sage, rabbitbrush, Apache Plume and hawthorn are planted. These are very xeric and tolerate the extreme road base conditions while providing a suitable screen for privacy, enclosure, wind protection and wildlife forage.

PROVIDING DIVERSITY: Gayle leaves the gardens untrimmed until spring to provide winter forage for wildlife. The landscape is dotted with bird and butterfly houses, nesting pouches, standing dead trees, sage and rabbitbrush, an ancient Piñon Pine and Utah Juniper trees. This delightful garden is also home to Henrietta the turkey. It was "thrill at first sight...since...turkeys always seemed to be the stuff of Plymouth Rock and the first Thanksgiving, not Basalt, Colorado." The first year the female turkey "browsed around...noshed" on birdseed and hunted worms in the lawn. The second year the female arrived paired with Mr. Tom and their many poults, and soon "novelty turned to nuisance" when Henrietta started to eat all the garlic and onion bulbs.

WILDSCAPING TIP: Deer seem to be the most frequent and persistent pests nibbling tender spring perennial shoots and prized peach blossoms. Gayle tried tufts of human hair, Irish Spring® soap, cayenne pepper spray and Deer Away®. Finally, fencing around certain plant specimens proved most effective. Gayle feels people should exhibit a more relaxed attitude when plant-eating insects and deer, berry-stealing birds, and pollinating bees appear. She suggests not becoming so "armed and alarmed."

FAVORITE PLANT: Rabbitbrush and Big Sage, Purple and native Yellow Coneflower, chokecherry and Mountain Gooseberry.

Monitoring & Troubleshooting

Walk through your Wildscape often to see what's working and what isn't:

- Are your plants leggy or overgrown? Maybe you're over-watering.

- Are the birds using the feeders and nest boxes? If not, relocate them. The guidelines are general and flexible, since birds don't read books!

- Are you covering the soil yearly with protective mulch? Not every site needs this, but many do.

- Are you seeing and enjoying new wildlife species? Are you keeping a list to share?

- Are your plants hampered by too much shearing and control? If yes, relax a bit if you're trying to create a welcoming habitat; let your plants go free to ramble and sprawl!

- A misplaced plant? Planting beds too overgrown? Transplant as necessary, but do all your transplanting during the cooler months of spring and fall (except at higher elevations), and make sure to leave the plants plenty of room to grow.

- Throughout the growing season, cut back dead blooms to encourage fresh growth; in the fall, keep the seed heads for bird food.

- Check weekly for pests and disease problems: early detection is easier to control. Remember that chewed up leaves are often the sign of a healthy yard: a munching caterpillar often turns into a butterfly

- Weekly weeding: listen to the birds chirping as you pluck the unwanted invaders.

- Take seasonal photos, then review to see if the overall design is pleasing to you. Do you have year-round color and variety? Are there spaces that need filling in?

If your heart delights

At the antics of a chickadee...

If a little toad winks as you pass by

Or you wish he would...

– Gwen Frostic, *A Place on Earth*

Then Wildscaping is for you!

5

KIDS, COMMUNITY AND THE CONTINUING WILDSCAPE ADVENTURE

Enjoying Your Wildscape

One of the marvels of a backyard wildscape is that it can serve as a constant source of wonder and fascination for every member of the family. No one is too young or too old to discover a wellspring of joy and discovery in the wildscape that's right outside their door. And this nearby wild is the key to truly re-connecting people with nature. You and your children don't necessarily have to carry out a structured activity in order to make your own discoveries. But many people have enjoyed a variety of special activities that are ideally suited for exploring wildscapes, no matter where they may be found. Some of these are par-ticularly suited for children, although they appeal to grown-ups, too! Wildscaping also works at the community level - helping people connect to nature and better connect with others in their own community.

Below are some activities and pursuits that you or someone in your family might like to try as a way to immerse yourself in the wildscape that you're creat-ing. Maybe these will suggest to you some other kinds of exploration that you'll want to pursue. What's important is that you don't miss out on the continuing adventure that awaits you in the natural world all around your home.

Calvin and Hobbes ©1992 & 1995 Watterson. Reprinted with permission of Universal Press Syndicate. All rights reserved.

Backyard Activities for Kids of All Ages

Kids of any age can play an important part in maintaining wildlife diversity by learning about the wild creatures in their backyard wildscapes, in the schoolyard, and in nearby natural areas. Knowledge leads to appreciation and can instill a deeper understanding and respect for the ways of nature. Rachel Carson wrote in *The Sense of Wonder*, "If a child is to keep alive his inborn sense of wonder...he needs the companionship of at least one adult who can share it, rediscovering with him the joy, excitement and mystery of the world we live in."

Getting to know birds and their behavior. Steven Saffier

Rock 'n Roll

Look for any rocks, logs or fallen branches in your wildscape. Gently roll the rock or log over and you'll discover a small city: a tiny community of insects, slugs and worms. Count how many different critters you see before they scamper back to safety and darkness. Count how many seconds it takes for them to hide from view. Handle them carefully and then slowly replace the roof of their home!

Science Lab

Take a family outing in the backyard and go sleuthing. With a bug box, capture caterpillars and other creepers and really look at their tiny adaptations. Count how many different birds you see, figure out which plants they feed and hide in, and listen to their calls. Be still and count how many different sounds beyond traffic noise that you hear. Keep a seasonal record and find out who's where when!

Birding

Your wildscape surely has feathered visitors. How are they spending their time out there? Why do nuthatches scurry down the trunk of a tree? Why does that little yellow bird flit so quickly from branch to branch? The answers are clues that will help you identify specific species of birds. Beyond their beautiful feathers and songs, bird behavior is a fascinating window into the world of birds and evolution.

In the spring, listen for what Terry Tempest Williams in *Refuge* described as "the way [bird's] songs begin and end each day - the invocations and benedictions of Earth." You can easily learn to discern the various songs and calls you hear - play bird tapes on those dark winter days to remind you that your wildscape is just resting, ever awaiting the renewal of life that Spring brings.

One of the best tools for becoming familiar with all the wild creatures is a field guide - if not of birds, then maybe insects or the stars. What's important is that you begin to see beyond just a tree or a bush - to sense the changes of seasons without a calendar and to know a new bird song when it echoes from your wildscape.

Growing A Habitat Gardener

It's never too early to nurture a budding habitat hero. Preschoolers love to dig holes and catch caterpillars. Kinder-gardeners love to build hideaways and play make-believe. At this age, a dead tree stump really requires in-depth snooping into the teeming micro world of insects. Elementary school kids get wonderstruck over bugs and pond creatures. With the school age progression, habitat wildscaping can make the connection between books and nature explorations.

Let your children pick a section of the garden and then let them choose plants or seeds that are fun

School children enjoying their tactile senses. Cathryn O'Connor

and easy to grow: Sunflowers grow almost before your eyes and their perky yellow heads follow the sun's rays from dawn to dusk. In the fall, the sunflower stalks are heavy with birds picking off every last seed. Fuzzy Wooly Thyme has a ticklish texture and offers nectar for the local bees. Herbs like dill are deliciously aromatic and a temporary home for the Black Swallowtail caterpillar - what fun to find them crawling among the stalks!

Keeping A Nature Journal

A creative way to increase interest in wildscaping is to maintain a Nature Journal. For example, the following journal page from Susie Mottashed's *Who Lives In Your Backyard?* shows one way to observe, sketch and record what's going on outside. Sketching what you see - whether or not you're an artist - inspires you to discover, record, and draw the everyday events in the lives of birds, insects, mammals, and plants that live nearby.

No matter the age - 5 to 95 - your observation skills will improve; your sketches will capture that perfect moment in time; and your creative spirit can come out and play! And you do not need any prior drawing skills - just an insatiable need to embrace the world around you.

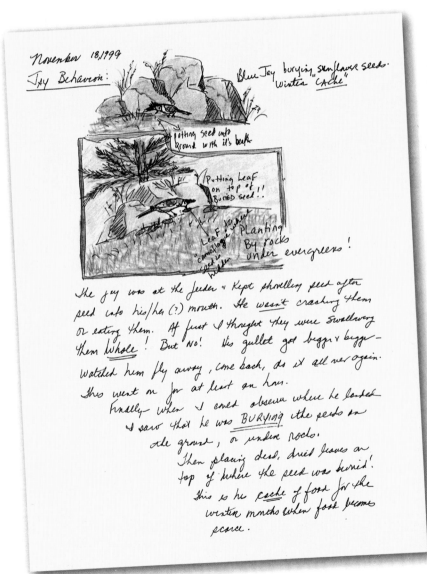

A Journal Page from Susie Mottashed's book Who Lives In Your Backyard?

Getting Involved in the Community

The preceding pages introduced you to the Audubon At Home vision for your own backyard. Now we want to expand this concept to include neighborhoods, communities and natural places. We want to create a "culture of conservation" in which people in all communities take an active role in conservation and eagerly embrace the role of stewardship.

Touch, Smell & Listen!

A family outing to the Audubon Center at Chatfield will delight the senses. The Audubon Society of Greater Denver has designed gardens that create wildlife habitats that are really living field guides, featuring native plant species and organic gardening methods. A butterfly garden provides shelter for eggs, food for growing caterpillars and nectar for the adults. The bird garden provides a variety of foods - berries, seeds and insects - as well as water and shelter.

The habitat gardens include a children's sensory trail for parents and toddlers - allowing tactile pleasures of sight, smell, sound and touch. Penstemons and Blanket Flowers create fun patterns, shapes and hues. Gently rubbing the leaves of yarrow, Fringed Sage and Nodding Onion fills the air with tantalizing scents. Visitors pause to eavesdrop on the wind rustling through the tall grasses and seedpods. Fingers experience textures from soft, fuzzy Pussytoes and Prickly Mock-Cucumber fruits.

Let's work together to create more community sensory gardens. Contact us via email: *aahcolorado@audubon.org*

Colorado Life Zones in the Schoolyard!

It's a short trip outside for students at Niwot Elementary School when they participate in the Science Garden Projects. Second graders might learn about seeds and collect samples from a variety of plantings. Third graders learn about and do composting, identify compost critters and plant a spring garden utilizing their ready-made compost. Fourth graders learn about Colorado's Life Zones both in the classroom and in the Science Garden.

A 4th grade Science class in the schoolyard learning about Colorado Life Zones. Cathryn O'Connor

These Life Zones begin in the Grasslands Zone with plants such as penstemon, Blanket Flower and Prairie Coneflower among the native grasses. The Foothills Zone highlights Smooth Sumac, One-seeded Juniper, Colorado Blue Spruce, Piñon Pine and Mountain Mahogany. A rise in grade leads to the Montane Zone, which meanders through the middle of the garden and includes plants such as currant, Ninebark, Kinnikinnick and Common Juniper. The Montane Zone is linked with the Riparian Zone, highlighting Rocky Mountain Alder and birch, aspen, willow and Red-stem Dogwood. The Sub-Alpine Zone, though difficult to duplicate on the Plains, grows Limber Pines and Bristle Cone Pines. The Alpine Zone features alpine plants such as Moss Campion, Alpine Forget-me-not and sedges all tucked in among well-placed boulders.

All this exciting class work on 1/3 acre! The planning and construction was completed by volunteer parents and teachers, and 2006 will bring a special 20th anniversary celebration of nature's cycles and Life Zones.

Wouldn't it be a great idea to have this program in all the schools - an exciting companion to the Audubon Adventures resources? Contact us via email: *aahcolorado@audubon.org*

Xeriscape Demonstration Garden in Pueblo West

With the assistance of the Utilities Director for Pueblo West, several newly certified Master Gardeners united a group of gardeners to create a garden design for a xeric demonstration garden at the Water Treatment Plant. Highlights from the garden, a work in progress, include planting beds devoted to CSU/Denver Botanic Gardens' Plant Select varieties, ornamental and native grasses, cacti and succulents, penstemons and assorted perennials.

Penstemons abound in this arid demo landscape: Pineleaf, Scarlet Bugler, Sand and Dusty varieties. Bob Johnson

They also conduct a yearly workshop on Xeriscaping. "It is not possible to read a newspaper or watch a news program without seeing something about...water shortages...A Xeriscape landscape is an ecologically sound investment by conserving water, reducing chemical usage and preserving native species. We do hope to excite you about the possibilities and whet your appetite to discover more." (Habitat Hero, Pueblo West)

The Pueblo West garden is an encouraging model of responsible activism in the community. Partner with Audubon Colorado to turn your neighborhood or community into a natural Xeriscape/Wildscape habitat.

Creating a Sense of Community in Steamboat Springs

Private donors and public participants partnered with the City of Steamboat Springs to create the Yampa River Botanic Park Association - a place of serenity celebrating the trees, shrubs, plants and birds of the Yampa River Basin. Its aim is to further the conservation and study of plants native to northwest Colorado.

The partnership transformed a six-acre, flat, horse pasture situated in the floodplain into 50 diverse microhabitats with man-made hills, streams, ponds, wetlands, and planting berms. Ranging from an aspen glade planted with Colorado Blue Columbines to hummingbird and butterfly gardens and waterwise gardens, the Botanic Park is now home to an exciting array of species including Great Blue Herons, Yellow-bellied Sapsuckers, sage-grouse, Rose-breasted Grosbeaks, and many other species.

The Botanic Park is truly a community effort: groups adopted many of the microhabitats and volunteers maintain the grounds; concerts and weddings are held there; local landscapers use it to teach new clients about plants. The Board of Directors is made up of community members as well as members from local civic organizations and the City.

The Yampa River Botanic Park is a heartwarming example of people working in partnership to create "a living environmental classroom resource for the greater community."

Does this give you any ideas for your own community? If so, contact Audubon Colorado via email: *aahcolorado@audubon.org*

Yampa River Botanic Park: Once an open pasture, this wild-scape sparkles with colorful plantings and abundant birdlife.
Bob Johnson

Citizen Science

Once you've created a wildscape in your backyard, the next thing you'll want to do is to see how successful it is in attracting and sustaining native birds and other wildlife. You may also want to know how your yard fits into the network of backyard wildscapes that are developing all across Colorado. Audubon At Home in Colorado will initiate an Internet-based Citizen Science Monitoring Program focused on quantifying the diversity and abundance of birds visiting backyard and neighborhood gardens in Colorado. Until this Monitoring Project is up and running, there are a couple of other Citizen Science activities that you can participate in right now, and right in your own backyard:

Great Backyard Bird Count

The GBBC is a four-day Citizen Science program held each President's Day weekend. It involves people counting birds in their yards and elsewhere, submitting their results online, and seeing their results displayed along with those of others. Audubon developed and runs this program with our partner, the Cornell Lab of Ornithology. The GBBC is a family-oriented, enjoyable and simple Citizen Science activity for people of all levels of experience and expertise. Participants enjoy watching birds, keeping a checklist, and submitting their sightings online to a central website (*www.birdsource.org*). They can view lists of birds seen in their local area, and compare their results with those of other birdwatchers. This is the perfect science-based activity for you and your family to do in your own backyard wildscape.

eBird

eBird is a web-based, place-based checklist program that provides individuals with the means to contribute to a collective and intricately detailed memory of the birds they see, again as a collaborative program of Audubon and Cornell. Individuals can keep track of their own backyard checklists over time and build a database of information on the bird activity in their wildscape from year to year.

For more information on these and other Audubon Citizen Science programs, visit the Audubon website at: *www.audubon.org*

End of Guide Book...Beginning of Your Wildscape Adventure

Thank you for your interest in Audubon At Home and we hope this is the beginning of your adventure in wildscaping, welcoming wild creatures to your gardens and daily lives. We hope that this guide has inspired you to create your own personal wildscape and thus, to bring conservation home to your yard and community. Help us create a culture of conservation in Colorado that will enrich not just our lives, but the lives that share these landscapes with us. Preserving healthy habitat is good for us all; welcoming wildlife brings nature up close, allowing us to take part in the web of life that surrounds each one of us.

Visit us at *www.auduboncolorado.org* for breaking wildscape news and tips, and to share your own wildscape adventures. We look forward to hearing from you.

6

COLORADO WILDSCAPE REGIONS
Learning Your Wildscape Zip Code

Review the following wildscape region descriptions and discover which best characterizes the natural landscape where you live. Remember that regions overlap where they meet, sometimes in very broad zones. Becoming familiar with the dominant elements of each wildscape region will enable you to make the best of your wildscaping opportunities and can make the difference between success and frustration. Each wildscape region has an accompanying Habitat Hero story telling how they are finding wildscaping success in that region.

Wildscape Regions Map of Colorado

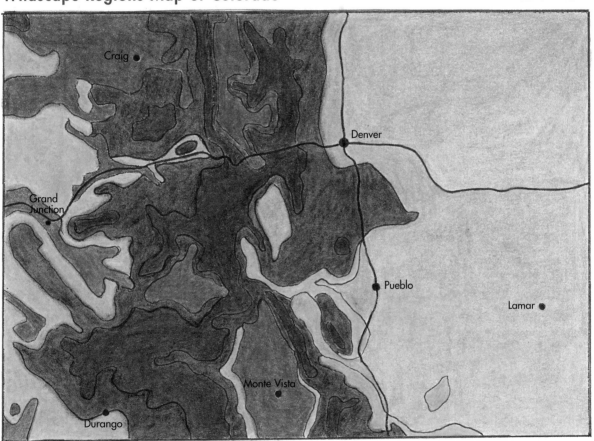

Modified after Explore Colorado..A Naturalist's Notebook, 1995.

▢ Plains Grassland		▢ Ponderosa Pine Forest	
▢ Semi-Desert Shrubland		▢ Spruce/Fir/Aspen Montane	
▢ Piñon-Juniper Woodland			

Pueblo County - Plains Grassland Bob Johnson

Pueblo, *eastern Colorado Springs, Denver, Boulder below the foothills, Greeley, and Fort Collins, as well as Sterling, Burlington and Lamar, all fall within the Plains Grassland Wildscape Region.*

Plains Grassland Wildscape Region

Ranging from roughly 3,000 to 5,500 feet elevation, this largely treeless region includes the eastern plains, where short grasses like Blue Grama and Buffalograss dominate and low-growing, drought resistant plants such as Plains Yucca, prickly pear cactus and Prairie Coneflower thrive. Trees cannot survive here outside of riparian areas without supplemental water. The plains are windy year-round, scorching in the summer, blustery cold in the winter; and they experience dramatic day-to-night temperature swings. The scant precipitation comes mainly in spring snows and summer thunderstorms.

Many areas within this region have been so altered by human settlement that they are barely recognizable as plains grasslands. Most Front Range cities, which were established on naturally occurring grassland east of the foothills, now support lush urban forests of trees and shrubs - the result of extensive irrigation of our yards and parks. But don't be fooled: when you wildscape in this region, you are contending with the basic conditions of the plains.

Plains grasslands are rich in wildlife, including songbird species such as the Horned Lark and Lark Bunting, many of which sing on the wing and nest on the ground. A number of our rarer bird species are found here, too, including the Mountain Plover and both the Greater and Lesser Prairie Chicken. Burrowing Owls inhabit prairie dog burrows, along with rattlesnakes and literally dozens of other species. Jackrabbits, Coyotes, and Swift Fox also call these grasslands home.

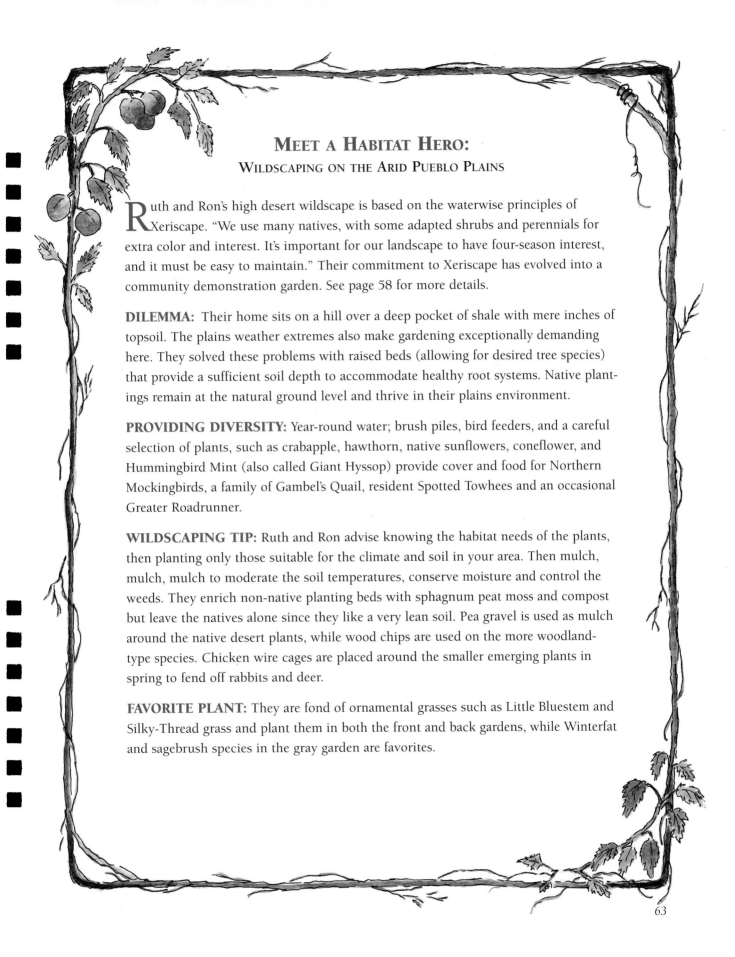

MEET A HABITAT HERO:
WILDSCAPING ON THE ARID PUEBLO PLAINS

Ruth and Ron's high desert wildscape is based on the waterwise principles of Xeriscape. "We use many natives, with some adapted shrubs and perennials for extra color and interest. It's important for our landscape to have four-season interest, and it must be easy to maintain." Their commitment to Xeriscape has evolved into a community demonstration garden. See page 58 for more details.

DILEMMA: Their home sits on a hill over a deep pocket of shale with mere inches of topsoil. The plains weather extremes also make gardening exceptionally demanding here. They solved these problems with raised beds (allowing for desired tree species) that provide a sufficient soil depth to accommodate healthy root systems. Native plantings remain at the natural ground level and thrive in their plains environment.

PROVIDING DIVERSITY: Year-round water; brush piles, bird feeders, and a careful selection of plants, such as crabapple, hawthorn, native sunflowers, coneflower, and Hummingbird Mint (also called Giant Hyssop) provide cover and food for Northern Mockingbirds, a family of Gambel's Quail, resident Spotted Towhees and an occasional Greater Roadrunner.

WILDSCAPING TIP: Ruth and Ron advise knowing the habitat needs of the plants, then planting only those suitable for the climate and soil in your area. Then mulch, mulch, mulch to moderate the soil temperatures, conserve moisture and control the weeds. They enrich non-native planting beds with sphagnum peat moss and compost but leave the natives alone since they like a very lean soil. Pea gravel is used as mulch around the native desert plants, while wood chips are used on the more woodland-type species. Chicken wire cages are placed around the smaller emerging plants in spring to fend off rabbits and deer.

FAVORITE PLANT: They are fond of ornamental grasses such as Little Bluestem and Silky-Thread grass and plant them in both the front and back gardens, while Winterfat and sagebrush species in the gray garden are favorites.

Delta County - Pinon-Juniper Woodland Jane Anderson

Walsenburg, Trinidad, Hotchkiss and Salida are among the towns located within the Piñon-Juniper Woodland Wildscape Region.

Piñon-Juniper Woodland Wildscape Region

These patchy woodlands dominate dry foothills and mesas between 5,000 and 8,000 feet elevation throughout southern Colorado, and northward at mid-elevations on the western slope to the Wyoming border, plus a few isolated places on the northern Front Range. Juniper trees dominate the stunted canopy of these woodlands at the lower end of the elevation range and Piñon Pines dominate at the upper edge, with a mix of the two in between. Intermingled with the P-J Woodlands are extensive thickets of Gambel's Oak, a shrubby oak that forms dense, head-high chaparral on steep slopes.

These are truly arid habitats, with the most reliable precipitation falling in spring and summer. Bunchgrasses like Needle-and-Thread, Blue Grama, and Junegrass dot bare ground, along with annual and perennial wildflowers, including Pallid Evening Primrose, Sidebells and Scarlet Bugler Penstemons. Birds frequenting this habitat include Black-chinned and Calliope Hummingbirds, Green-tailed Towhees, flocks of Piñon Jays, and Juniper Titmice, Black-throated Gray Warblers, and Bushtits. It is also home to the highest diversity of lizards and snakes in Colorado.

MEET A HABITAT HERO:
HELPING WILDLIFE IN HOTCHKISS

Jane gardens because it brings her "closer to the earth physically and mentally. My landscape is for the birds and me mostly. I really like the wildlife that a good friendly landscape attracts and want to help them live on in this human-controlled world."

DILEMMA: Construction trucks tracked weed seeds onto her very dry sagebrush hillside. Jane solved the infestation by "seed reduction" - getting on all fours and pulling weeds before they set seed, then planting natives. One of her successes: Rocky Mountain Beeplant, which flowers all summer long without being watered and provides nectar for bees, butterflies, and hummingbirds.

PROVIDING DIVERSITY: Junipers attract many of the 57 bird species that visit the yard and provide cover for the seed feeders. Three bluebird houses have yet to be occupied by bluebirds since the Ash-throated Flycatcher chases them away every spring. All the dry sagebrush in the natural landscape doubles nicely as brush piles. Blue Grama seed is great junco and sparrow food, while hawthorn berries and Crabapple provide abundant winter food. Three-leaf Sumac has red-yellow fruit that could be a bird attractant if the branch tips weren't browsed by deer.

Jane, "with lots of help," made a rock-strewn streambed and small pond in her courtyard that attracts water-seeking birds. She feels that this oasis attracts as many birds as her feeders, berries, seeds and flowers. Salamanders and water striders are now residents.

WILDSCAPING TIP: Deadheading old blossoms (i.e., pinching off blooms when they start to fade) pays off in prolonged flowering; but when fall approaches, let them go to seed for the sparrows and juncos. For economical water usage, Jane suggests adding organic matter to the soil before planting, and to not poison the insects - they are bird food!

FAVORITE PLANT: Jane's favorite hummingbird plant is Red-Birds-in-a-Tree (native to the high Chihuahuan desert and available through mail order nurseries), and she is beginning to appreciate the longevity and reseeding of Rocky Mountain Penstemon in comparison to other short-lived species. She is also on her third Desert Beard Tongue, since it is so beautiful at age three with its bright pink bloom, though that is also the time when it begins to die off.

Pueblo County - Ponderosa Bob Johnson

Ponderosa Pine Forest Wildscape Region

Pagosa Springs, *Woodland Park, Buena Vista, Conifer, and Estes Park are located in the Ponderosa Pine Forest Wildscape Region. The Front Range foothills south of Denver to Trinidad, the area around Durango in southwestern Colorado, and Glenwood Springs all fall within the area dominated by shrub communities.*

This savanna-like forest region characterizes the foothills and mountains from 5,500 to 9,000 feet elevation above the arid shrublands and woodlands and below the wetter mountain forests. Stands of these drought-tolerant and fire-resistant pines dominate the foothills west of Denver, the Upper Arkansas River Valley, and portions of southwestern Colorado. Most of this region's precipitation comes from late winter and spring snowfall.

A diverse variety of shrubs, grasses, and wildflowers thrive in the understory beneath mature Ponderosa Pines, including Gambel's Oak, Kinnickinnick and Snowberry, Idaho Fescue and King Fescue, and Scarlet Gilia and Lewis' Flax. Year-round birds found in this wildscape region include Great Horned Owls, Steller's Jays, Hairy and Lewis' Woodpeckers, White-breasted and Pygmy Nuthatches, Mountain Chickadees and Pine Siskins. Summer brings migrants such as Violet-green Swallows, Williamson's Sapsuckers, Flammulated Owls, and Broad-tailed Hummingbirds.

Where soils in the Ponderosa region are compact clay instead of well-drained, Gambel's Oak, Mountain Mahogany, Serviceberry and other shrubs dominate instead of the tall pines, with Douglas-fir appearing on cooler exposures. The varied and abundant seeds, fruits and berries of this unique habitat make it a mecca for at least 50 species of mammals, such as Abert's Squirrels, and over 70 species of birds, including Pygmy Nuthatches.

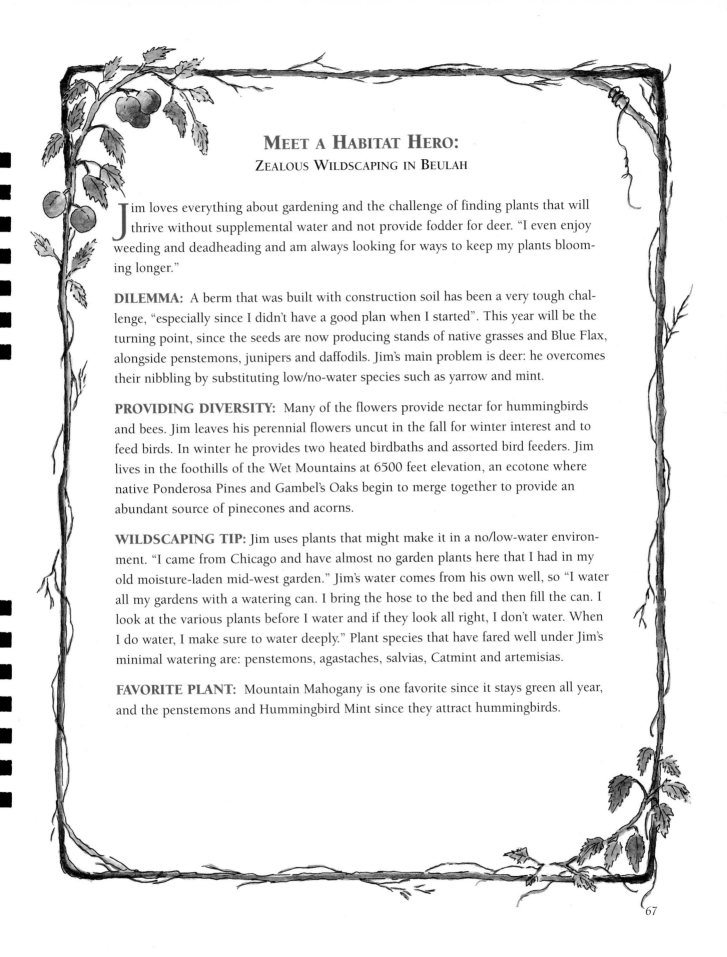

MEET A HABITAT HERO:
ZEALOUS WILDSCAPING IN BEULAH

Jim loves everything about gardening and the challenge of finding plants that will thrive without supplemental water and not provide fodder for deer. "I even enjoy weeding and deadheading and am always looking for ways to keep my plants blooming longer."

DILEMMA: A berm that was built with construction soil has been a very tough challenge, "especially since I didn't have a good plan when I started". This year will be the turning point, since the seeds are now producing stands of native grasses and Blue Flax, alongside penstemons, junipers and daffodils. Jim's main problem is deer: he overcomes their nibbling by substituting low/no-water species such as yarrow and mint.

PROVIDING DIVERSITY: Many of the flowers provide nectar for hummingbirds and bees. Jim leaves his perennial flowers uncut in the fall for winter interest and to feed birds. In winter he provides two heated birdbaths and assorted bird feeders. Jim lives in the foothills of the Wet Mountains at 6500 feet elevation, an ecotone where native Ponderosa Pines and Gambel's Oaks begin to merge together to provide an abundant source of pinecones and acorns.

WILDSCAPING TIP: Jim uses plants that might make it in a no/low-water environment. "I came from Chicago and have almost no garden plants here that I had in my old moisture-laden mid-west garden." Jim's water comes from his own well, so "I water all my gardens with a watering can. I bring the hose to the bed and then fill the can. I look at the various plants before I water and if they look all right, I don't water. When I do water, I make sure to water deeply." Plant species that have fared well under Jim's minimal watering are: penstemons, agastaches, salvias, Catmint and artemisias.

FAVORITE PLANT: Mountain Mahogany is one favorite since it stays green all year, and the penstemons and Hummingbird Mint since they attract hummingbirds.

Eagle County - Montane Mary Pownall

Leadville, *Fairplay, Aspen, Vail, Frisco, and Winter Park are located in the Spruce/Fir/Aspen Montane Wildscape Region.*

Spruce/Fir/Aspen Montane Wildscape Region

Ranging roughly from 8,000 to 11,500 feet elevation, this wildscape region is the general habitat of ski country. Winters are long, snowfall is heavy, and summer is short but spectacular, since plants bloom all at once in dazzling displays during the short growing season, and birds and other animals pack their breeding activities into the few weeks available. On sunny south-facing slopes, such as those in Eagle County, sagebrush and other shrubs dominate even at high elevations, while dense forest and aspen groves typify shady north-facing slopes, such as above Vail Village.

Clark's Nutcrackers and Ruby-crowned Kinglets are common throughout, while layers of dense understory provide good breeding grounds for Warbling Vireos, Northern Flickers, Mountain Bluebirds, Western Tanagers and Cordilleran Flycatchers. Extensive aspen groves support Northern Goshawk nests.

Refer to the plant lists beginning on page 74 for recommended hardy, high elevation selections.

MEET A HABITAT HERO:
MOIST WILDSCAPING IN VAIL VILLAGE

Mary gardens for the beauty it brings into the world and her life. "I also do volunteer work at Betty Ford Alpine Gardens because I believe in their mission of showing the community what can be grown in a difficult climate."

Blue Columbine
© Wendy Shattil/Bob Rozinski

DILEMMA: At 8200 feet, a steep roadside slope dotted with aspen and Colorado Blue Spruce has been turned into a shade-dappled garden, bright with Iceland Poppies, Painted Daisies and fluttering Tibetan prayer flags. The garden is buried under deep snow a lot of the year, but early April brings nodding daffodils and crocuses. As the snow recedes in May, Snowdrops and Bloodroot carpet the slope with long-overdue color. In most years, flowering continues into early November with pansies and deadnettle.

PROVIDING DIVERSITY: A mountain stream traversing the landscape provides lots of soil moisture for Marsh Marigolds and the occasional American Dippers. Various nest boxes host an array of birds, and a Violet-green Swallow inside and an American Robin on top mutually shared one box this year.

WILDSCAPING TIP: In early spring before bears come out of hibernation, Mary top-dresses her garden with 50-pound bags of fish and cottonseed meal to enrich her mountain soil. She does highly recommend that the nutrients be put down well before the bears appear, since they find the fishy meal to their liking, especially when a pail of meal was inadvertently left out on the porch.

FAVORITE PLANT: An unusual primrose that will grow in partially shady conditions, Orchid Primrose (native to China) with dark fuchsia buds opening to pinkish blooms...lovely!

Mesa County - Semi-Desert Shrubland   Jim Knopf

Semi-Desert Shrubland Wildscape Region

Alamosa, *Gunnison, Grand Junction, and Rangely are among the towns located in the Semi-Desert Shrubland Wildscape Region.*

Ranging from the state's lowest elevations around 3,500 feet to as high as 8,500 feet, this region occurs in the lowest parts of the Western Slope around Grand Junction, and also at higher elevations in mountain parks that lie in the rain shadow, such as around Gunnison, North Park, and the San Luis Valley. This wildscape region is the driest in Colorado, and the hottest as well; the lower elevations experience Colorado's longest frost-free seasons.

Shrublands are, by definition, treeless and range from the extensive areas of sagebrush in the mountain parks - home to the state's two species of sage-grouse and many other bird species - to the alkaline soils of the west slope and the San Luis Valley, which support Four-winged Saltbush, Shadscale, and Greasewood. Four hummingbird species use the Semi-Desert Shrublands, along with a host of other wildlife species, ranging from horned lizards to Swainson's Hawks, which hunt the shrublands for grasshoppers and rodents.

MEET A HABITAT HERO:
DESERT DIVERSITY IN GRAND JUNCTION

Lee and Teri feel that even though plants do not communicate with us, you can often tell what their needs are, almost as though they were talking. Like us, they are living beings, but they don't always do well in human-dominated landscapes.

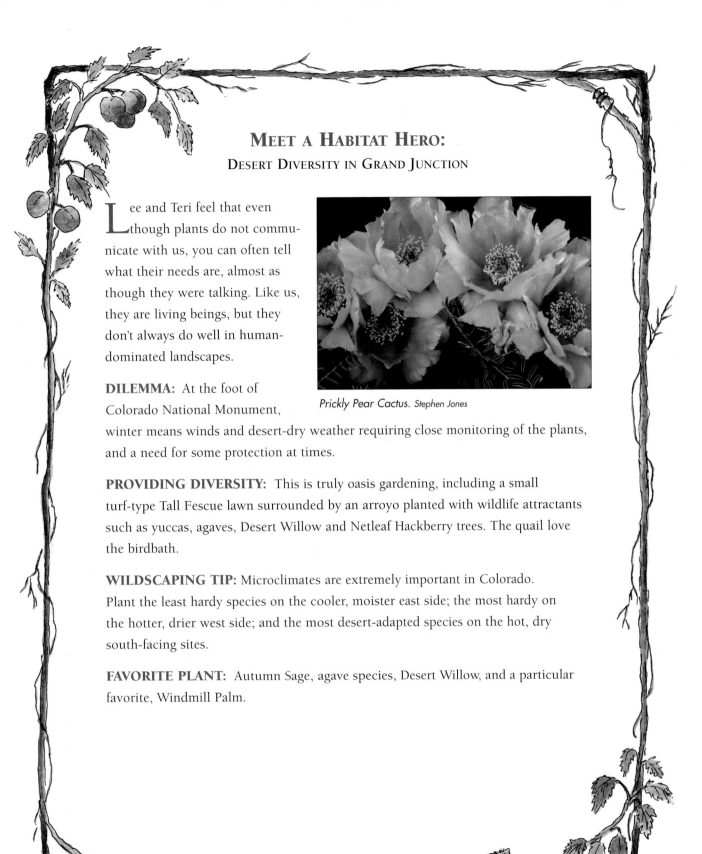

Prickly Pear Cactus. Stephen Jones

DILEMMA: At the foot of Colorado National Monument, winter means winds and desert-dry weather requiring close monitoring of the plants, and a need for some protection at times.

PROVIDING DIVERSITY: This is truly oasis gardening, including a small turf-type Tall Fescue lawn surrounded by an arroyo planted with wildlife attractants such as yuccas, agaves, Desert Willow and Netleaf Hackberry trees. The quail love the birdbath.

WILDSCAPING TIP: Microclimates are extremely important in Colorado. Plant the least hardy species on the cooler, moister east side; the most hardy on the hotter, drier west side; and the most desert-adapted species on the hot, dry south-facing sites.

FAVORITE PLANT: Autumn Sage, agave species, Desert Willow, and a particular favorite, Windmill Palm.

Restoration of a ditch into a willowy neighborhood creek in Salida has attracted dippers and other riparian wildlife showing what is possible with wildscaping. Chaffee County - Willowy Creek Susan J. Tweit
Plant photos: City of Boulder OSMP
Dipper: Bill Schmoker

Numbers towns *and cities, including Denver, La Junta, Telluride, Craig, and Steamboat Springs, are located in, adjacent to, or straddling a Riparian/Wetlands Wildscape Zone.*

Riparian/Wetlands Wildscape Zone

Riparian and wetland areas, such as ponds, marshes, streams, rivers, lakes and playas, are not a separate region by themselves; rather, they are sprinkled throughout all the wildscape regions of the state. These habitats are crucial for wildlife, with as many as 80% of Colorado's wild species depending on wetlands at some stage of their life. Yet they make up less than 2 percent of Colorado landscapes. They are also the most endangered of Colorado's habitats. Restoration or creation of a wetland or stream, if appropriate for your site, will grace your life with an abundance of wildlife.

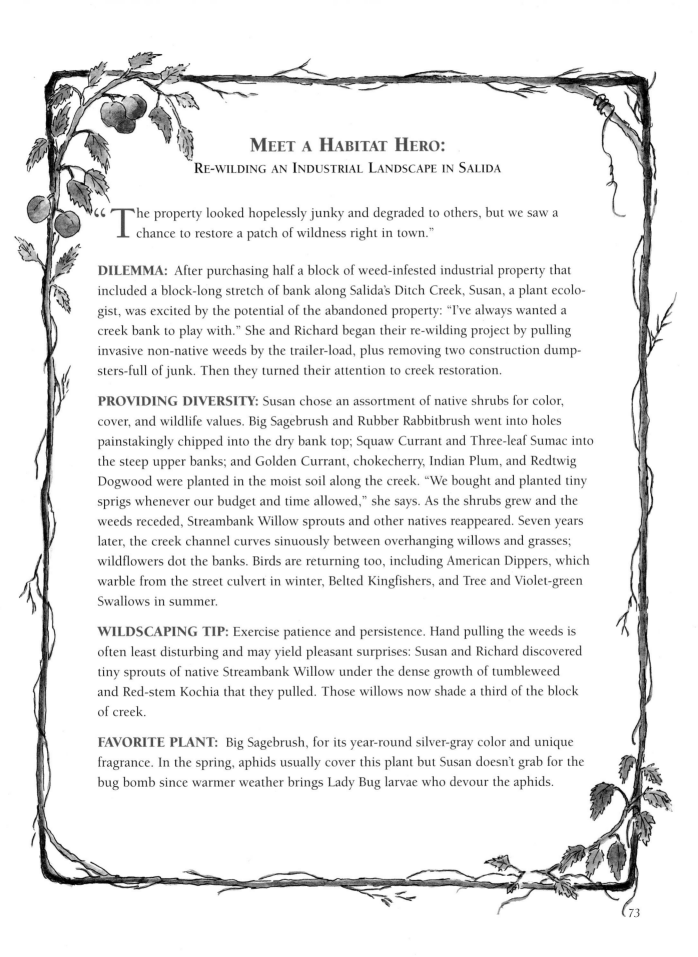

MEET A HABITAT HERO:
RE-WILDING AN INDUSTRIAL LANDSCAPE IN SALIDA

"The property looked hopelessly junky and degraded to others, but we saw a chance to restore a patch of wildness right in town."

DILEMMA: After purchasing half a block of weed-infested industrial property that included a block-long stretch of bank along Salida's Ditch Creek, Susan, a plant ecologist, was excited by the potential of the abandoned property: "I've always wanted a creek bank to play with." She and Richard began their re-wilding project by pulling invasive non-native weeds by the trailer-load, plus removing two construction dumpsters-full of junk. Then they turned their attention to creek restoration.

PROVIDING DIVERSITY: Susan chose an assortment of native shrubs for color, cover, and wildlife values. Big Sagebrush and Rubber Rabbitbrush went into holes painstakingly chipped into the dry bank top; Squaw Currant and Three-leaf Sumac into the steep upper banks; and Golden Currant, chokecherry, Indian Plum, and Redtwig Dogwood were planted in the moist soil along the creek. "We bought and planted tiny sprigs whenever our budget and time allowed," she says. As the shrubs grew and the weeds receded, Streambank Willow sprouts and other natives reappeared. Seven years later, the creek channel curves sinuously between overhanging willows and grasses; wildflowers dot the banks. Birds are returning too, including American Dippers, which warble from the street culvert in winter, Belted Kingfishers, and Tree and Violet-green Swallows in summer.

WILDSCAPING TIP: Exercise patience and persistence. Hand pulling the weeds is often least disturbing and may yield pleasant surprises: Susan and Richard discovered tiny sprouts of native Streambank Willow under the dense growth of tumbleweed and Red-stem Kochia that they pulled. Those willows now shade a third of the block of creek.

FAVORITE PLANT: Big Sagebrush, for its year-round silver-gray color and unique fragrance. In the spring, aphids usually cover this plant but Susan doesn't grab for the bug bomb since warmer weather brings Lady Bug larvae who devour the aphids.

7

RESOURCES

Wildlife Friendly Native Plants by Wildscape Region

(H denotes hardy, high elevation survivors)

PLAINS GRASSLAND

Common Name	Scientific Name	Notes
Grasses		
Indian Grass	*Sorghastrum avenaceum*	Winter seed source/H
Little Bluestem	*Schizachyrium scoparium*	Winter seed source/H
Side Oats Grama Grass	*Bouteloua curtipendula*	Nectar and seed source
Switchgrass	*Panicum virgatum*	Cover and fall color
Perennials		
Bush Sunflower	*Helianthus pumilus*	Fall seed source
Stemless Evening Primrose	*Oenothera howardii*	Lures hovering moths
Orange Butterflyweed	*Asclepias tuberosa*	Butterfly magnet/H
Prairie Coneflower	*Ratibida columnifera*	Finches eat seed heads
Yellow Prickly Pear	*Opuntia polyacantha*	Bee nectar; fruit
Shrubs		
Hackberry	*Celtis reticulata*	Fruit eaten by birds
Hawthorn	*Crataegus erythropoda*	Fruit, thorns for cover
Sand Cherry	*Cerasus (Prunus) besseyi*	Every one eats the fruit
Three Leaf Sumac/Skunkbush	*Rhus aromatica ssp. trilobata*	Fruit for birds
Trees		
Plains Cottonwood	*Populus deltoides/monilifera*	Nest habitat for orioles & owls

PINON-JUNIPER WOODLAND

Common Name	Scientific Name	Notes
Grasses		
Blue Grama	*Chondrosum bouteloua gracilis*	Substitute for bluegrass/H
Indian Ricegrass	*Achnatherum hymenoides*	Seeds eaten by birds/H
Needle and Thread	*Hesperostipa comata*	Seeds eaten by birds/H
Perennials		
Wild Four O'clock	*Mirabilis multiflora*	Nectar feeding insects
Rocky Mountain Bee Plant	*Cleome serrulata*	Butterfly magnet/self sows
Rocky Mountain Penstemon	*Penstemon strictus*	Nectar feeding insects
Scarlet Bugler Penstemon	*Penstemon barbatus*	Hummingbird attractant
Silvery Lupine	*Lupinus argenteus*	Seeds eaten by birds/H
Shrubs		
Oregon-Grape	*Mahonia repens*	Berries eaten by birds
Rubber Rabbitbrush, Green	*Chrysothamnus nauseosus*	Moths, butterflies, birds/H
Three-leaf Sumac	*Rhus aromatica trilobata*	Berries and cover/H
Trees		
Piñon Pine	*Pinus edulis*	Pinon Jays/wildlife eat nuts
Rocky Mountain Juniper	*Sabina scopulorum*	Winter berries/birds/H

PONDEROSA PINE FOREST/GAMBEL'S OAK CHAPARRAL

Grasses

Big Bluestem	*Andropogon gerardii*	Winter seed source
Idaho Fescue	*Festuca idahoensis*	Seeds eaten by birds
Junegrass	*Koeleria macrantha*	Cover, food for grazers/H
Mountain Muhly	*Muhlenbergia montana*	Cover/food for birds

Perennials

Bee Balm	*Monarda fistulosa*	Hummer magnet/self sows
Scarlet Gilia	*Ipomopsis aggregata*	Hummingbird magnet
Sulfur Flower Buckwheat	*Eriogonum umbellatum*	Butterflies and bees
Wild Strawberry	*Fragaria virginiana ssp. glauca*	Fruit eaten by everyone

Shrubs

Boulder Raspberry	*Oreobatus (Rubus) deliciosus*	Fruit eaten by wildlife
Kinnikinnick	*Arctostaphylos uva-ursi*	Berries eaten by wildlife
Mountain Ninebark	*Physocarpus monogynus*	Showy blooms/seed/H
Mountain Mahogany	*Cercocarpus montanus*	Cover/pods/birds
Serviceberry	*Amelanchier alnifolia*	Fruit eaten by wildlife/H
Silver Buffaloberry	*Shepherdia argentea*	Fruit eaten by wildlife

SPRUCE/FIR/ASPEN MONTANE

Grasses

Mountain Muhly	*Muhlenbergia montana*	Cover/food for birds

Perennials

Tall Beard Tongue, Blue Mist	*Penstemon virgatus*	Hummingbirds and butterflies
Colorado Columbine	*Aquilegia caerulea*	Bee magnet
Coral Bells	*Heuchera sanguinea*	Nectar feeding insects
Western Sneezeweed	*Helenium hoopesii*	Bird and insect food

Shrubs

Mountain Spiraea	*Holodiscus dumosus*	Cover for birds
Red Elderberry	*Sambucus racemosa*	Every one eats the berries
Thimbleberry	*Rubacer parviflorus*	Fruit for wildlife
Twinberry Honeysuckle	*Lonicera involucrata*	Cover, nectar and berries

Trees

Aspen	*Populus tremuloides*	Woodpecker/swallow nesting

SEMI-DESERT SHRUBLAND

Grasses

Bluebunch Wheatgrass, Western	*Agropyron spicatum*	Good cover, birds eat seeds
Idaho Fescue	*Festuca idahoensis*	Bunchgrass, birds eat seed
Saltgrass	*Distichilis stricta*	salty soils okay, birds eat seed

Perennials

Adobe Blanketflower	*Gaillardia pinnatifida*	Birds eat seeds, nectar/bees
Arrowleaf Balsamroot	*Balsamorhiza sagittata*	Bee magnet, birds eat seeds
Indian Paintbrush	*Castilleja integra*	Hummer magnet/buy seed
Lewis' Flax - Blue	*Linum lewisii*	Butterfly/bee/not European var.
Prince's Plume	*Stanleya pinnata*	Spring nectar bees/hummers
Silvery Lupine	*Lupinus argenteus*	Birds eat the seeds/H

Shrubs

Antelope Bitterbrush	*Purshia tridentata*	Birds eat the seeds
Big Sagebrush	*Artemisia tridentata*	Cover for birds and lizards
Four-winged Saltbush	*Atriplex canescens*	Seeds/leaves eaten, good cover
Winterfat	*Krascheninnikovia lanata*	Stellar winter browse plant

Trees

Utah Juniper	*Sabina osteosperma*	Berries eaten by birds

RIPARIAN/WETLANDS

Grasses/Grasslike plants

Cattail	*Typha latifolia*	Cover/nest material/spreads
Prairie Cordgrass	*Spartina pectinata*	Cover and seeds
Tufted Hairgrass	*Deschampsia caespitosa*	Cover and seeds/H

Perennials

Arrowhead	*Sagittaria latifolia*	Cover, nectar for insects
Nuttall's Sunflower	*Helianthus nuttallii*	Goldfinches love seeds
Rocky Mountain Iris	*Iris missouriensis*	Nectar for spring insects

Shrubs

Chokecherry	*Padus (Prunus) virginiana*	Bees, all eat the fruit/H
Golden Currant	*Ribes aureum odoratum*	Flowers attract hummers, bees
Peach Leaf Willow	*Salix amygdaloides*	Cover
Redtwig Dogwood	*Cornus stolonifera*	Cover, birds eat berries
Streambank Willow, Coyote	*Salix exigua*	Cover

Sources: City of Boulder Open Space and Mountain Parks, Colorado Native Plant Society, The Nature Conservancy, Susan J. Tweit

Wildscape Notes

Plant List for Species Used in the Text

Native and non-native plants mentioned in the text are listed alphabetically by their common name, followed by the scientific name. The Notes section lists bloom color, growing conditions, wildlife value such as seeds, nectar, fruit, and (H) for hardy, higher elevation survivors. Name in ( ) denotes alternative common name.

Common Name	Scientific Name	Notes
Agave, Perry & New Mexico	*Agave parryi, neomexicana*	Hot/dry/sun/bees/hummers
Antelope Bitterbrush	*Purshia tridentata*	Yellow/dry/south facing/birds/H
Apache Plume	*Fallugia paradoxa*	Rose like blooms/sun/dry
Artemisia	*Artemisia 'Powis Castle'*	Silver lacy mound/woody/hardy
Artemisia, Silver King	*Artemisia ludoviciana var. albula*	Silver foliage/dry/hot
Ash, Mountain	*Sorbus scopulina*	White/red fruit/moist/birds/H
Aspens, Quaking	*Populus tremuloides*	Best at higher elevations
Asters	*Aster species*	Native species preferred
Aster, Golden	*Heterotheca villosa*	Yellow/dry/spreading habit
Beard Tongue	Penstemon species	Sand/gravelly/no organic mulch
Beard Tongue, Desert	*Penstemon pseudospectabilis*	Hot pink/dry/hot/hummers
Beard Tongue, Tall (Blue Mist)	*Penstemon virgatus*	Purple/part sun/moist/hummers/H
Bee Balm	*Monarda didyma*	Purplish/fragrant/hummers/bees
Bell's Twinpod	*Physaria bellii*	Yellow/dry/rock garden
Black-eyed Susan	*Rudbeckia hirta*	Yellow/sun/dry/butterflies
Blanket Flower	*Gaillardia aristata*	Yellow/ sun/ dry/moth
Blue Flax, Lewis	*Linum lewisii*	Dry/sun/by seed
Blue Grama	*Chondrosum gracilis*	Turf/dry
Bloodroot	*Sanguinaria canadensis*	Pinkish clump/moist/H
Bluestem, Big	*Andropogon gerardii*	Silver-red fall foliage
Bluestem, Little	*Schizachyrium scoparium*	Blue leaves/red fall foliage
Boulder Raspberry	*Rubus deliciosus*	White/edible fruit /H
Buckwheat, Shasta sulfur	*Eriogonum umbellatum*	Yellow/sun/dry/butterflies
Buffaloberry, Silver	*Shepherdia argentea*	Good thorny hedge/fruit/birds
Buffalograss	*Buchloe dactyloides*	Turf/dry/below 7000 feet
Butterflyweed	*Asclepias tuberosa*	Orange/clay/H
California Poppy	*Eschscholzia californica*	Yellow/sun/dry/reseeds
California Fuchsia		See Hummingbird Trumpet
Campanula, Blue	*Campanula lasiocarpa*	Basal tuft/sandy/rock garden
Catmint	*Nepeta x faassenii*	Blue/sun/H
Chocolate Flower	*Berlandiera lyrata*	Yellow/fragrant/dry
Chokecherry	Padus *(Prunus) virginiana*	White/fruit/moist/wildlife/H
Cinquefoil, Leafy	*Drymocallis fissa*	Yellow/dry/rock gardens
Cinquefoil, Shrubby	*Potentilla fruticosa*	Creamy/very adaptable
Clematis, Sweet Autumn	*Clematis terniflora*	White/cool roots/good cover
Columbine, Colorado	*Aquilegia caerulea*	Bluish/moist/partial sun/H
Coreopsis	*Coreopsis grandiflora*	Yellow/long bloom/sun
Cotoneaster	*Cotoneaster species*	Good cover & hedge
Cottonwood, Lanceleaf	*Populus x. acuminata*	Moist/butterflies/male only
Cottonwood, Plains	*P. deltoides ssp. monilifera*	Moist/don't plant male

Common Name	Scientific Name	Notes
Crabapple, Sargent	*Malus sargentii*	White/small fruit/wildlife
Crabapple, Japanese Flowering	*Malus floribunda*	Fire blight resistant/small fruit
Currant, Golden	*Ribes aureum*	Yellow/fragrant/berry/birds
Currant, Red Prickly	*Ribes montigenum*	White/berry/moist/high elevation
Currant, Wax (Squaw)	*Ribes cereum*	Pinkish/dry
Datura, Sacred (Angel's Trumpet)	*Datura innoxia*	White/night/poisonous
Delphinium	*Delphinium grandiflorum*	Blue/biennial/hummers
Desert Four-O-Clock	*Mirabilis multiflora*	Purple/dry/sun
Double-Bubble Mint (Hyssop)	*Agastache cana*	Rose/sun/dry/hummers
Douglas Fir	*Pseudotsuga menziesii*	Evergreen/tall tree/H
Elderberry, Red	*Sambucus racemosa*	White/red fruit/moist/birds/H
Elderberry, American	*Sambucus canadensis*	White/berries for everyone/H
Elm	*Ulmus species*	Yellow fall foliage
Fernbush	*Chamaebatiaria millefolium*	Creamy/fernlike leaves/dry/bees
Fescue, Idaho	*Festuca idahoensis*	Blue-green/tight bunch
Fescue, Sheep	*Festuca ovina*	Mid height bunchgrass
Fescue, Tall	*Festuca arundinacea*	Mod-low water turf type
Fleabane, Trailing Aster	*Erigeron compositus*	White daisy like/sun
Fringed Sage, Wormwood	*Artemisia frigida*	Yellow/dry/sun/fragrant
Fireweed	*Epilobium angustifolium*	Pink/moist/nectar/bees
Four-winged saltbush	*Atriplex canescens*	Silvery/good in salty soils
Gayfeather, Dotted	*Liatris punctata*	Purple/dry/sun/butterflies
Gazania	*Gazania linearis*	'CO. Gold'/sun/self sow
Golden Banner	*Thermopsis divaricarpa*	Yellow/moist/part sun
Goldenrod, Stiff	*Oligoneuron rigida*	Yellow/moist/by seed
Gooseberry, White Stemmed	*Ribes inerme*	Pink/moist/wildlife
Grape Holly, Creeping	*Mahonia repens*	Low spreading habit/H
Grape, Oregon	*Mahonia aquifolium*	'Compacta'/berries/shade
Greasewood	*Sarcobatus vermiculatus*	Good in salty soils
Hackberry, Netleaf/Western	*Celtis reticulata*	Yellowish/red fruit/dry/wildlife
Hackberry, Common	*Celtis occidentalis*	Fruit for birds/very hardy
Hawthorn	*Crataegus erythropoda*	White/red fruit/thorns/dry
Hawthorn, Thornless Cockspur	*Crataegus crus-galli inermis*	White/red fruit/ tough/hardy
Hummingbird Mint/Hyssop	*Agastache rupestris*	Red-orange/minty/sun/dry
Hummingbird Trumpet	*Zauschneria garrettii*	Orange/low/rich soil/hummers
Indian Ricegrass	*Achnatherum hymenoides*	Seed/dry/ornamental/H
Iris, Rocky Mountain Wild	*Iris missouriensis*	Purplish/part sun/moist
Junegrass	*Koeleria macrantha*	Turf/dry/H
Juniper, Rocky Mountain	*Sabina juniperus scopulorum*	Evergreen/fruit/dry/wildlife
Juniper, Utah	*Juniperus osteosperma*	Evergreen/high desert
Jupiter's Beard (Valerian)	*Centranthus ruber*	Red/sun/butterflies
Kinnikinnick, Bearberry	*Arctostaphylos uva-ursi*	White-red fruit/semi-dry/H
Lamb's Ear	*Stachys byzantina*	Wooly white leaves/purple/
Lamium (Dead Nettle)	*Lamium maculatum*	White or yellow/dry/shade
Leadplant	*Amorpha canescens*	Blue/dry-clay/sun/butterflies

Common Name	Scientific Name	Notes
Maple, Rocky Mountain	*Acer glabrum*	Seeds/moist/shrubby/H
Maple, Silver	*Acer saccharinum*	Fall color/moist soils
Marsh Milkweed	*Asclepias incarnata*	Wet/butterflies
Marigold, Desert	*Baileya multiradiata*	Yellow/dry/hot/perennial
Mexican Hat, Coneflower	*Ratibida columnifera*	Red or yellow/dry
Mock Cucumber	*Echinocystis lobata*	Ornamental vine
Moonflower	*Ipomoea alba*	Heart shaped white/night/fragrant
Mountain Mahogany	*Cercocarpus montanus*	Creamy/feathery pods/dry/H
Nanking Cherry	*Prunus tomentosa*	White/shrub/edible fruit
Needle-and-Thread Grass	*Hesperostipa comata*	Feathery seed head/bunch/H
Ninebark, Mountain	*Physocarpus monogynus*	Pinkish cluster/fall color
Nodding Onion	*Allium cernuum*	Ornamental, fragrant
Oak, Burr	*Quercus macrocarpa*	Tolerates clay soils/wildlife
Oak, Gambel's (Scrub)	*Quercus Gambelii*	Shrubby/sprouts/wildlife
Oak, Pin (Swamp)	*Quercus palustris*	Sandy soil/acorns
Painted Daisy	*Tanacetum coccineum*	Varied/bushy/sun
Palm, Windmill	*Trachycarpus fortunei*	Tolerates light frost
Penstemon, Blue Mist	*Penstemon virens*	Blue-violet/part sun/dry
Penstemon, Dusty	*Penstemon cammarhenus*	Purplish/xeric/sun/H
Penstemon, Pineleaf	*Penstemon pinifolius*	Red or yellow/hardy/hummers/H
Penstemon, Rocky Mountain	*Penstemon strictus*	Blue/moist/sun or part sun/
Penstemon, Sand	*Penstemon ambiguus*	White/xeric/sun
Penstemon, Scarlet bugler	*Penstemon barbatus*	Red spikes/self sows/ hummers
Penstemon, Sidebells	*Penstemon secundiflorus*	Blue-purple/dry/hot
Pincushion Flower	*Scabiosa columbaria*	Lilac/sun/annual/butterflies/H
Pine, Bristlecone	*Pinus aristata*	Evergreen/seeds/wildlife
Pine, Piñon	*Pinus edulis*	Evergreen/seeds/everyone
Pine, Ponderosa	*Pinus ponderosa ssp. scopulorum*	Evergreen/seeds/wildlife/H
Plum, Wild/Indian	*Prunus americana*	White/fruit/moist/wildlife/H
Poppy, Iceland	*Papaver nudicaule*	Varied hues/short lived
Prairie Clover, Purple	*Dalea purpurea*	Evergreen/dry/self sows
Prairie Coneflower	*Ratibida columnifera*	Yellow/sun/dry
Prairie Cordgrass	*Spartina pectinata*	Ornamental/dry
Prickly Pear Cactus	*Opuntia polyacantha*	Yellow/fruit/dry/sun/wildlife
Primrose, Asian	*Primula vialii*	Pink/fuchsia/ shade
Primrose, Evening Stemless	*Oenothera howardii*	Yellow/dry/sun/moth
Primrose, White Evening	*Oenothera caespitosa*	White/sun/dry/fragrant
Prince's Plume	*Stanleya pinnata*	Yellow spikes/gravel/sun
Privet, New Mexico (Olive)	*Forestiera neomexicana*	Shrubby hedge/lots of seed/birds
Pussy Toes	*Antennaria parvifolia*	Pinkish/forms large mats/dry
Rabbitbrush (Tall Green)	*Chrysothamnus graveolens*	Yellow/sun/dry/butterflies
Rabbitbrush (Dwarf Blue)	*C. nauseosus nauseosus*	Bluish foliage/dry/sun
Red-Birds-in-a-Tree	*Scrophularia macrantha*	Red spike/dry/hummers
Redtwig Dogwood	*Cornus stolonifera*	White/scarlet stems/moist
Rocky Mountain Bee Plant	*Cleome serrulata*	Pinkish/dry/sun/butterflies
Rose, Wild	*Rosa woodsii*	Pink/sun/dry/thickets

Common Name	Scientific Name	Notes
Rose, Wild	*Rosa woodsii*	Pink/sun/dry/thickets
Sage, Autumn	*Salvia greggii*	Magenta/hot/dry/hummers
Sage, Silver mound	*Artemisia 'Powis castle'*	Silvery/mounding form
Sagebrush, Big (Western)	*Artemisia tridentata*	Silvery/fragrant/dry/butterflies
Saltbush, Shadscale	*Atriplex confertifolia*	Silvery/salty soils/butterflies/birds
Salvia	*Salvia nemorosa*	Purple/long bloom/ butterflies
Sandcherry, Western	*Prunus besseyi 'Pawnee Buttes'*	White/dry/fruit/fall color
Scarlet Gilia	*Ipomopsis aggregata*	Scarlet/dry/self sows/moth
Sedges	*Carex species*	Wet/seed heads
Serviceberry, Saskatoon	*Amelanchier alnifolia 'Regent'*	White/edible fruit/fall color/H
Shooting Star	*Dodecatheon pulchellum*	Buy seeds/rich soils
Side-oats Grama Grass	*Bouteloua curtipendula*	Attractive bloom/dry/butterflies
Silky-thread Grass	*Stipa neomexicana*	Southern plains areas only
Snowberry, Mountain	*Symphoricarpos oreophilus*	White/berries/shrub/H
Snowdrops	*Galanthus species*	Bulb/white/moist rock gardens
Spiraea Western	*Spiraea douglasii*	White clusters/moist
Spruce, Colorado Blue	*Picea pungens*	Evergreen tree/moist/H
Sumac, Smooth	*Rhus glabra*	Reddish/velvety fruit/Front Range
Sumac, Three Leaf (Skunkbush)	*Rhus aromatica ssp. trilobata*	Yellow/red fruit/dry/birds
Sunflower, Nuttall's	*Helianthus nuttallii*	Yellow/seed/moist/birds
Sunset Hyssop	*Agastache rupestris*	Red-orange/minty/sun/dry
Switchgrass	*Panicum virgatum*	Ornamental
Thyme, Wooly	*Thymus lanuginosus*	Gray leaf mat, fragrant, bees
Trumpet Creeper Vine	*Campsis radicans*	Orange/sun/lean soils/hummers
Twinberry Honeysuckle	*Lonicera involucrata*	Reddish/moist/fruit and nectar/H
Verbena, Scarlet	*Verbena x hybrida*	Sun/hummer and butterflies
Viburnum, Highbush Cranberry	*Viburnum edule*	Whitish/red berries & foliage/H
Viburnum, Cranberrybush	*Viburnum trilobum compacta*	Fruit & foliage/wildlife
Virginia Creeper	*Parthenocissus quinquefolia*	Fruiting vines/fall foliage/birds
Willow, Desert	*Chilopsis linearis*	Purple/dry/hot/small tree/hummers
Willow, Streambank	*Salix exigua*	Silvery/wet/butterflies
Winecups, Poppy Mallow	*Callirhoe involucrata*	Magenta/spreading/clay
Winterfat	*Ceratoides lanata*	Silvery/sun/sandy soil/seeds
Yarrow, White Wooly	*Achillea millefolium lanulosa*	White/part sun/nectar
Yarrow, Moonshine	*Achillea taygetea*	Yellow/dry/long blooms/H
Yucca, Adam's Needle	*Yucca filamentosa*	White/sun/dry/moths
Yucca, Banana	*Yucca baccata*	White/sun/dry/moths
Yucca, Plains	*Yucca glauca*	Creamy/sun/dry/moths

Wildscape Notes

Information Resources

Audubon Colorado
1966 13th Street
Boulder, CO 80302
303-415-0130
www.auduboncolorado.org

National Audubon Society
700 Broadway
New York, NY 10003
212-979-3000
www.audubon.org

Colorado Audubon Chapters:
Aiken Audubon Society
P.O. Box 76987
Colorado Springs, CO 80970
Vaughanphoto@pcisys.com

Arkansas Valley Audubon Society
P.O. Box 11187
Pueblo, CO 81001
seettamoss@hotmail.com

Audubon Society of Greater Denver
9308 South Wadsworth Blvd.
Littleton, CO 80128
303-973-9530
info@denveraudubon.org

Black Canyon Audubon Society
P.O. Box 1371
Paonia, CO 81428
bday@tds.net

Boulder County Audubon Society
P.O. Box 2081
Boulder, CO. 80306
www.boulderaudubon.org

Evergreen Naturalists Audubon Society
P.O. Box 523
Evergreen, CO 80437
david3drb@netscape.net

Fort Collins Audubon Society
P.O. Box 271968
Fort Collins, CO 80527
5mcorp@virenet.com

Grand Valley Audubon Society
P.O. Box 1211
Grand Junction, CO 81502
970-241-4670
info@audubongv.org

Platte & Prairie Audubon Society
30 S. Fremont
Johnstown, CO
sharpek@ucar.edu

Roaring Fork Audubon Society
P.O. Box 1192
Carbondale, CO 81623
birder@rof.net

San Juan Audubon Society
7125 CR 203
Durango, CO 81301

Stephen Jones

Organizations:

Betty Ford Alpine Gardens
Vail, CO 81657
970-476-0103
www.bettyfordalpinegardens.org

Colorado Native Plant Society
P.O. Box 200
Fort Collins, CO 80522
www.conps.org

Colorado State University
Cooperative Extension
Master Gardener Program
9595 Nelson Road
Longmont, CO 80503
303-776-4865
www.coopext.colostate.edu

Denver Botanic Gardens
1005 York Street
Denver, CO 80206
720-865-3500
www.botanicgardens.org

Denver Water
Xeriscape
1600 W 12th Avenue
Denver, CO 80204
303-628-6000
www.denverwater.org

Green Industries of CO.
9367 W Vandeventor Dr.
Littleton, CO 80128
303-973-4026
www.greenco.org

Lady Bird Johnson Wildflower Center
Austin, TX
512-292-4100
www.wildflower.org

The Nature Conservancy
1881 Ninth Street
Boulder, CO 80302
303-444-2950
Natives & Invasive Weeds
www.tnc.org

Western Colorado Botanical Garden
and Butterfly House
641 Struthers Avenue
Grand Junction, CO 81501
970-245-3288
www.wcbotanic.org

Yampa River Botanic Park
Steamboat Springs, CO 80477
970-879-4300
www.steamboatsprings.net

Government Contacts:

City of Boulder,
Open Space & Mountain Parks
P.O. Box 791
Boulder, CO 80306
303-441-3440
www.ci.boulder.co.us/openspace/

USDA Natural Resources Conservation Service
Backyard Conservation
www.nrcs.usda.gov
National Plant List
http://plants.usda.gov

U. S. Environmental Protection Agency
Pesticides
www.epa.gov/pesticides/

Some Native Plant Sources Recommended by Colorado Gardeners:

Brady's Garden Center
1121 S. 9th Street
Canon City, CO 81212
719-275-1286

Chelsea Nursery
3347 G Road
Clifton, CO 81520
970-434-8434

Cliffrose High Desert Gardens
27885 Highway 160
Cortez, CO 81321
970-565-8994

Flower Bin
1805 Nelson Road
Longmont, CO 80501
303-772-3454

Fort Collins Nursery
2121 E. Mulberry
Fort Collins, CO 80524
970-482-1984
www.fortcollinsnursery.com

Harlequin's Gardens
4795 N 26th Street
Boulder, CO 80301
303-939-9403
www.harlequinsgardens.com

Harding Nursery
Colorado Springs, CO
719-596-5712
www.hardingnursery.com

High Country Gardens
2902 Rufina Street
Santa Fe, NM 87507
800-925-9387
www.highcountrygardens.com

Hudson Gardens
6303 S. Santa Fe Dr.
Littleton, CO 80120
303-797-8565
www.hudsongardens.org

Planted Earth
12744 Highway 82
Carbondale, CO 81623
970-963-1731
www.plantedearth.com

Pleasant Avenue Nursery
506 South Pleasant Ave.
Buena Vista, CO 81211
719-395-6955

Ramshorn Native Plants
Box 881810
Steamboat Springs, CO 80488
970-276-4448

Rocky Mountain Native Plants
3780 Silt Mesa Road
Rifle, CO 81650
970-625-4769

Sunscapes Nursery
330 Carlisle Avenue
Pueblo, CO 81004
719-546-0047
www.sunscapes.net

Timberline Gardens
11700 W 58th Avenue
Arvada, CO 80004
303-420-4060
www.timberlinegardens.com

Western Native Seed
Box 188
Coaldale, CO 81222
719-942-3935
www.westernnativeseed.com

REFERENCES

Contributors:

Award-winning author and commentator Susan J. Tweit is a field ecologist who is in love with life in all its diverse forms. Her eight books include *Rocky Mountain Garden Survival Guide*, an easy-to-use primer on how gardens work.

Ann Green, Green Design, is an award-winning designer and art director who specializes in environmentally conscious publications for Rocky Mountain Nature Association, The National Parks and USDA Forest Service and National Audubon Society.

Susie Mottashed is a nature illustrator and author who teaches nature journaling workshops based on her new book, *Who Lives In Your Backyard?*. Her nature and bird illustrations appear in the Boulder County Audubon and Boulder Bird Club newsletters.

Jim Knopf is a landscape architect specializing in Rocky Mountain Xeriscape design and author of numerous waterwise landscaping books. He lectures and teaches classes on Xeriscaping throughout the area.

Connie Holsinger is the Project Coordinator for *Colorado Wildscapes* and an Audubon Colorado Board Member. She is President of The Terra Foundation and has coordinated similar wildscape projects in Massachusetts and Florida.

Gary Graham is Vice President and Executive Director of Audubon Colorado and has served as Senior Editor and Advisor for *Colorado Wildscapes*.

Ken Strom is Director of Bird Conservation of Audubon Colorado and has served as Technical Editor and Advisor for *Colorado Wildscapes*.

Bob Johnson has traveled the state photographing the Habitat Heroes' Wildscapes and is an Audubon Colorado Board Member.

Photographers: We give our thanks to the following people for allowing us to use their photos: Jane Anderson, Lynn and Bruce Bowen, Jim Hawkins, Stephen Jones, Panayoti Kelaidis of Denver Botanic Gardens, Jim Knopf, Cathryn O'Connor, Mary Pownall, Scott Severs, Bill Schmoker (*www.schmoker.org*), Wendy Shattil and Bob Rozinski, Gayle Shugars, Steven Saffier, Pearl Taylor, Dave Sutherland of City of Boulder OSMP and David Winger of Denver Water.

Acknowledgments: We thank all the people who have shared their time, interest and knowledge towards the realization of Colorado Wildscapes. In particular, we want to give special notice to Jessie Boyer for her Habitat Hero leads; Cathryn O'Connor, Volunteer Naturalist; Lisa Tasker, Colorado Native Plant Society; Anita Cote, Amy Schlotthauer and Joan Tweit for proofreading; Maggie Curran and Becky Eterno of The Flower Bin; Susan Smith of Denver Audubon; Don D'Amico and Dave Sutherland of City of Boulder OSMP; and Sally Conyne, Paul Green and Steven Saffier of National Audubon Science Office. We appreciate the principal funding provided by The Terra Foundation; and matching funding provided by Xcel Energy, Denver Water, Natural Resources Conservation Service, and McStain Neighborhoods.

Bibliography

A Place On Earth
Gwen Frostic
Presscraft Papers, 1973

*Best Perennials for the Rocky Mountains
And High Plains*
CSU Cooperative Extension
Bulletin 573A

Boulder County Nature Almanac
Ruth Carol Cushman, Stephen R. Jones,
Jim Knopf
Pruett Publishing Co., 1993

Colorado Gardener's Guide
John L. Cretti
Cool Springs Press, 1998

Explore Colorado...A Naturalist's Notebook
Frances Alley Kruger
Carron A. Meaney
Denver Museum of Natural History and
Westcliffe Publishers 1995

From Grassland to Glacier
Cornelia Fleischer Mutel and John C. Emerick
Johnson Books, Boulder 1992

Gardening in the Mountain West
Barbara Hyde
Johnson Printing, Boulder, 1999

National Audubon Society
Audubon At Home
www.audubon.org

National Audubon Society: The Bird Garden
Stephen W. Kress
DK Publishing, Inc. 1995

Native Plants for High-Elevation Western Gardens
Janice Busco & Nancy R. Morin
Fulcrum Publishing, 2003

Pollinator Conservation Handbook
Matthew Shepherd et al.
The Xerces Society, Portland, OR, 2003

Refuge: An Unnatural History of Family and Place
Terry Tempest Williams
Vintage Books, 1992

Rocky Mountain Garden Survival Guide
Susan J. Tweit
Fulcrum Publishing, 2004

The Silent Spring
Rachel Carson
Harper & Row, 1965

Sunset
Western Garden Book
Kathleen Norris Brenzel, Editor
Sunset Publishing, 2001

The Audubon Society Guide to Attracting Birds
Stephen W. Kress
Charles Scribner's Sons, 1985

Undaunted Garden
Lauren Springer
Fulcrum Publishing, 2000

Waterwise Landscaping with Trees, Shrubs & Vines: A Xeriscape Guide for the Rocky Mountain Region, California, and Desert Southwest
James Knopf
Chamisa Books, Boulder 2003

Who Lives In Your Backyard?
Susie Mottashed
Sketches from the Heart Publishing, 2004
www.sketchesfromtheheart.com

Xeriscape Plant Guide
Rob Proctor, Denver Water
Fulcrum Publishing, 1996

Xeriscape Colorado
Connie Lockhart Ellefson, David Winger
Westcliffe Publishers 2004

Audubon COLORADO

Join Today

By becoming a member of Audubon, you will receive a full year of membership benefits including the following:

- The award winning Audubon magazine
- Opportunities to participate in Audubon conservation campaigns
- Opportunities to engage with your local Audubon chapter
- Access to Audubon sanctuaries
- Access to travel opportunities domestically and internationally
- Invitations for workshops and ecology camps

You can join through our website *www.audubon.org* and select "Join Audubon" under the "Give Now" button. Your gift to Audubon is tax deductible except for the $15 fair market value of the magazine. Please allow 4-6 weeks for the arrival of your first issue.

Or please complete the form below and mail to:

Audubon Membership Data Center
P.O. Box 51003
Boulder, CO 80323

- *CUT HERE* -

Name_____Street Address_____

City/State/Zip_____E-mail (optional)_____

Membership Types:

USA: 1 Year $20_____ Canada: 1 Year $45US_____ International: 1 Year $50US_____

Credit Card Type: ☐ Visa ☐ Mastercard ☐ American Express

Credit Card Number: _____

Credit Card Expiration: _____

Wildscaping Up Close

Above: Cathryn O'Connor
Top and far right: Stephen Jones
Right: ©Wendy Shattil/Bob Rozinski
Bottom: Bob Johnson